Getting Started with

Windows™ 3.1

Getting Started with

Windows™ 3.1

**Russell Borland**

PUBLISHED BY
Microsoft Press
A Division of Microsoft Corporation
One Microsoft Way
Redmond, Washington 98052-6399

Library of Congress Cataloging-in-Publication Data
Borland, Russell, 1946–
    Getting started with Windows 3.1 / Russell Borland.
      p. cm.
    Includes index.
    ISBN 1-55615-472-0 : $19.95
    1. Microsoft Windows (Computer program)   I. Title.
QA76.76.W56B673   1992
005.4'3--dc20   92-4620
                                                CIP

Printed and bound in the United States of America.

1 2 3 4 5 6 7 8 9 AGAG 6 5 4 3 2 1

Distributed to the book trade in Canada by Macmillan of Canada, a division of Canada Publishing Corporation.

Distributed to the book trade outside the United States and Canada by Penguin Books Ltd.

Penguin Books Ltd., Harmondsworth, Middlesex, England
Penguin Books Australia Ltd., Ringwood, Victoria, Australia
Penguin Books N.Z. Ltd., 182–190 Wairau Road, Auckland 10, New Zealand

British Cataloging-in-Publication Data available.

CompuServe is a registered trademark of CompuServe, Inc. GEnie is a trademark of General Electric Corporation. HP and LaserJet are registered trademarks of Hewlett-Packard Company. Microsoft, Microsoft Press, MS-DOS, and XENIX are registered trademarks and Windows is a trademark of Microsoft Corporation. Arial and Times New Roman are registered trademarks of The Monotype Corporation PLC. UNIX is a registered trademark of UNIX Systems Laboratories. Paintbrush is a trademark of ZSoft Corporation.

Companies, names, and/or data used in screens and sample output are fictitious unless otherwise noted.

Acquisitions Editor: Michael Halvorson
Project Editor: Rich Gold
Technical Editor: Mary DeJong

To Capt. Spaulding,
Dr. Science,
and LAL

Contents

Part One: Learning Windows

Part Three: Using the Accessories in Windows

Acknowledgments

This book, like all others at Microsoft Press, required a team effort. Although I get my name on the cover and so am entitled to keep all the blame for deficiencies, I gladly acknowledge the contributions of the team that made this book better than I could have alone.

Editor Rich Gold expended enormous energy improving many sections of the book. I'm sure he really does feel like a zookeeper after his efforts. His dedication to usability testing paid off in many improvements to Part One. Technical editor Mary DeJong prodded, pulled, and nudged the fun-loving and fanciful lions of description into their proper and correct cages. Compositor Debbie Kem skillfully tamed herds of wild editorial marks.

Lani Lindell gave the zoo a colorful entrance (cover design). Kim Eggleston created a playful zoo garden (book design), while Peggy Herman performed wonderful feats of laying out the grounds (page design and production). Lisa Sandburg's artwork gave the zoo joyful signs and illustrations.

Principal proofreader Deborah Long made sure we didn't litter the play area with erroneous scraps and other verbal garbage. And once again, typographer Carolyn Magruder put the final shine on the zoo, getting it ready for opening day, with typography and page layout.

I also thank many unnamed members of the team for handling coordination, additional proofing, printing, manufacturing, distribution, marketing, and sales. No book ever gets to you without these people, who toil mostly anonymously for the greater good of the general reading public.

Introduction

With Microsoft Windows 3.1, you'll have more fun running a computer than you thought possible. Windows is pretty. Windows is easy. Windows is also, well, you know, useful.

The Windows operating system can be colorful, pleasing to the eye, and entertaining. And all the while you are being soothed, pleased, and entertained, you'll also get lots of work done, which can lead to pleasing results and rewards.

The Greatness of Windows

Chapter 1 is "Why Windows?" and it describes the world without Windows as a dark wilderness full of wild beasts. It describes the world with Windows as a well-lit zoological garden. Windows accomplishes this transformation not only by providing lots of tools (called *applications*) for doing different jobs but also by gluing the applications together so that they cooperate. All applications for Windows work similarly and can share information back and forth. As you learn to play with Windows, you'll soon realize why you want Windows and why you want to use Windows all the time.

How to Use This Book

This book was created for someone new to Windows who may also be new to computers. It takes a light-hearted but practical approach to learning to use Windows, focusing on the basics first, in fast-paced practical sessions, and then building on this foundation in later chapters.

In Part One, "Learning Windows," you'll cover the essentials. The information is presented sequentially, and you'll want to work through all the chapters in order. Among the basics, you'll learn how to play a game to help you learn to use the mouse and various features of Windows. You'll learn how to set up Windows to please your eye and to fit the way you like to work. By the end of Part One, you'll know just about all you need to know to plunge into any application for Windows.

Part Two, "Windows in More Depth," dances more dances with the main applications you learned about in Part One and that you will use to do essential tasks, such as starting applications, filing your work, and printing. The information you learn in Part Two will add polish to your use of Windows.

Part Three, "Using the Accessories in Windows," shows you how to use the accessories that come with Windows, including Write (a word-processing application for writing letters and reports), Calculator, Calendar, and Cardfile. You can read these chapters and explore these applications for Windows as you need them, in any order.

More Books You'll Want to Read

If, after you finish this book, you'd like to learn more about Windows, the following books can provide information about more advanced topics.

Concise Guide to Microsoft Windows 3.1 by Kris Jamsa. A summary of all Windows features. Published by Microsoft Press.

Windows 3.1 Companion by Lori L. Lorenz and R. Michael O'Mara with Russell Borland. A thorough introduction to every Windows feature. Doesn't overwhelm the reader with technical detail. A Cobb Group book, published by Microsoft Press.

Running Windows 3.1 by Craig Stinson. A comprehensive guide to every feature and secret of Windows, with lots of tips for efficient and advanced use of this operating system. Published by Microsoft Press.

Part One

Learning Windows

The chapters in Part One are intended to be read *sequentially*. They're short, enjoyable practices that build on one another to teach you the basic skills needed to use the Windows operating system.

Chapter 1

Why Windows?

You're trying to do your job. You're trying to have fun. You're trying to use your personal computer. Without the Windows operating system you're wandering in the wilderness at night. The computer screen is flat and black. You can't find the tools, supplies, or information you need. You can't see your way from where you are to the end of your journey. There are no road signs, no pictures, no visible organization. And deep down, you are apprehensive, feeling that some wild beast in your computer is going to take a bite out of your work.

Instead, enter Windows, which offers civilization and light. The dark wilderness with voracious beasts is transformed by Windows into a bright, well-marked zoological garden, a garden of iconographic delights.

To understand this transformation you first have to understand something more about the wilderness on your computer and the problems that Windows solves. Computers are literal and deliberate. Every task you want a computer to perform requires that you find and call upon a different *application* and give a specific set of commands. If you want to write a letter, you have to start a word processing application. When you want to draw a picture, you have to start a drawing application. And so on. Without Windows, you start and close these applications individually with unique sets of typed codes, and the applications themselves probably look very different from one another. You might have to use different sets of commands in the applications, even when they are performing similar tasks, like searching for files or copying information.

In the zoological garden of Windows, on the other hand, your applications are organized into groups of pictures so you can easily find them when you need them. The Windows location for these pictures is called *Program Manager,* and it's the first thing you see when you start Windows and the last thing you see when you quit. In between, you return to Program Manager to start another application. You can run lots of applications at the same time.

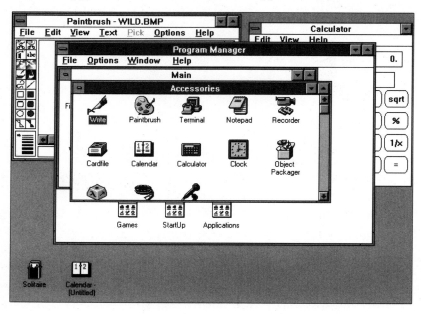

In the Windows operating system, you see everything inside windows. A window is a bordered area that you can resize and move around on the computer screen. In one application the window might be an area in which you play a game. In another application it might be an area in which you draw or read information or calculate your taxes. Often an application can have several working windows inside its application window, enabling you to compare versions of a report or transfer paragraphs from one report to another. You can even move information back and forth between different applications, transferring spreadsheet information (rows and columns of numbers) into the window of a tax return or transferring a drawing into the window of a written report. In every application the windows work similarly.

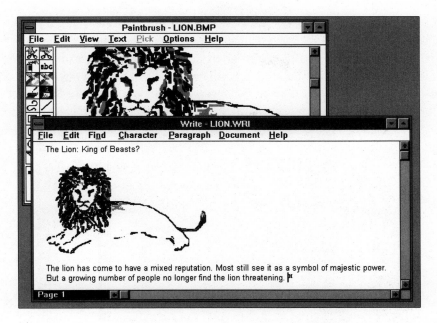

To make Windows even easier to use, you can manipulate what you see on the computer screen with a *mouse*. The mouse is a hand-held device connected to your computer to control the pictures on the screen. When you move the mouse on your desk, a pointer moves on the screen. If you move the pointer to certain pictures on the screen and then click the button on your mouse, you can make things happen. It's very easy and understandable. Not only can you use the mouse to locate and start your applications, you can also use it to open several windows, move windows, change their sizes, and switch between them.

One nice way that Windows tames the beasts in the computer wilderness is by making all applications in Windows work in pretty much the same way. Each application's window has *menus* of *commands*. You choose one of these commands to initiate an action, like selecting a new character font for a letter you're writing. Applications also have *dialog boxes* that pop up on the screen to give you information or to help you execute commands; for example, when you choose the Fonts command, a dialog box pops up to give you choices of font, style, and size.

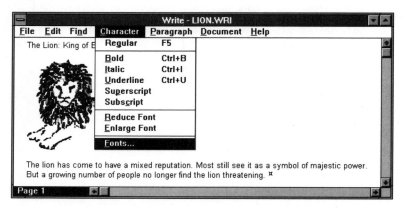

Not only does Windows help you do your work, it also helps you stay organized. With a tool called File Manager, Windows gives you an easy-to-use filing system. The documents you write, the pictures you draw, and the spreadsheets you create in various applications are displayed as pictures of files in File Manager. You can organize the files into folders, rename them, copy them, or throw them away.

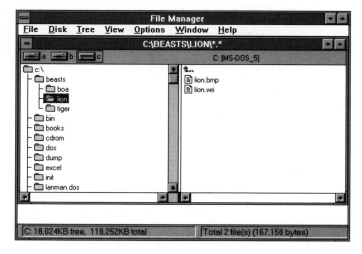

Windows makes life easier. It presents you with pictures and work spaces to help you perform your work and organize your files on a personal computer. It gives you easy ways to manipulate those pictures and work spaces. And Windows gives you a set of behaviors that are pretty consistent across lots of applications. You should have a pleasant saunter through the Windows zoological garden. It isn't perfect, but when you're new to computers, Windows can make you feel like today's picnicker rather than yesterday's lunch.

Chapter 2

Installing Windows

Before you can play with the Windows operating system, you have to install it on your computer. This chapter discusses the Windows Setup program that handles installation. If you already have Windows on your computer, you can skip this chapter and go directly to Chapter 3, ''Starting Out, Finding Your Way, and Quitting.'' You don't need the information between here and there.

RUNNING THE SETUP PROGRAM

To install Windows on your computer, insert Disk 1, *Setup*, in a floppy-disk drive. Type the disk drive's letter designation and a colon followed by the word *setup*. For example, if Disk 1 is in disk drive A, type

```
a:setup
```

Now press the Enter key to start the Windows Setup program.

> **NOTE** *Windows is a nice guy and adapts itself to your computer. The Windows Setup program checks out your computer and notes its type, the kind of display, the type of keyboard and mouse, and the network connections you have installed (if any). Even though it can be useful to you to know the type of equipment you have, don't worry if you don't know. You can be happy and confident that Windows knows.*

As the installation proceeds, the Windows Setup program displays instructions and offers choices. In most cases, all you have to do is press the Enter key to direct Windows Setup to continue. The Windows Setup program is very reliable for all popular and well-known computers, especially for computers that are fully compatible with IBM personal computers. If at any time you get stuck or don't understand what to do next, you can turn to the Windows Setup program for help. (See the information on F1 below.)

As the Windows Setup program tells you, you can get assistance at any time during the setup process. The Help system gives you information online (that is, it gives you screens of information right there on the computer), so you don't have to leave your work to look for a reference book. Just press the F1 key whenever you want Help information.

If you aren't sure how to control a setup program, you should press F1 at the first screen you see in the Windows Setup program. After you view the Help information, press the Esc key. You'll find yourself back at the first Windows Setup screen, ready to continue the setup process.

If you believe that the setup process has gone awry, you can exit the Windows Setup program at any time by pressing the F3 key. The F3 key exits the Windows Setup program. The Windows Setup program leaves your computer and hard disk the way they were before you started except that the information already copied to your computer is not erased. Of course, to use Windows, you'll have to install it completely by starting the Windows Setup program from the beginning.

Riding the Setup Express

The Windows Setup program first asks whether you want to use the Express Setup or the Custom Setup. Take the Express! Simply press the Enter key on your keyboard. After that, your main task will be to remove a floppy disk and insert the next when you're instructed to do so. (After you insert the new disk in the floppy-disk drive, remember to press the Enter key.) During installation, the Windows Setup program will also prompt you to type your name and specify the kind of printer you have.

If you have an earlier version of Windows on your computer, the Windows Setup program asks you where you want to store the new version. The proposed location is a directory named C:\WINDOWS. Leave this directory name as is, and press the Enter key.

Windows Tutorial

During installation, the Windows Setup program gives you the opportunity to try the Windows Tutorial. The Windows Tutorial has two parts: one that shows you how to use the mouse and one that introduces you to the basics of Windows. If you have never used a mouse before, run the Mouse lesson before you continue Windows Setup. Why? You need to understand and feel comfortable performing mouse operations like *clicks*, *double-clicks*, and *drags*. If these terms aren't part of your computer knowledge, the Windows Tutorial is just what you need. In addition, Chapter 4 of this book, "Using the Mouse," gives you instruction and practice in, well, using the mouse.

The Windows Basics lesson will give you a good start in learning how to use Windows. Go ahead and work your way through it. Don't worry about remembering all the details presented to you in the tutorial. The remaining chapters in Part One of this book discuss the basics and give you practice to help you remember what you learn.

FINISHING SETUP WITH MULTIPLE CHOICE

If you are installing Windows for the first time, Windows Setup ends with the box shown in Figure 2-1. You should choose the Reboot button by pressing the Enter key on your keyboard. This button restarts your computer so that it can use all the options that Windows Setup installed.

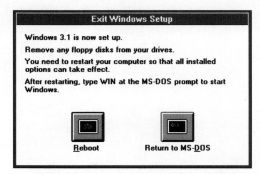

FIGURE 2-1. *The choices at the end of Windows Setup if you are installing Windows for the first time.*

If you are using Windows Setup to replace an earlier version of Windows on your computer, you may see either the box in Figure 2-1 or a different box, the one shown in Figure 2-2. Which box you see depends on whether you need to restart your computer to take full advantage of Windows Setup's changes to your computer, or not. If you see the box in Figure 2-1, press the Enter key to choose Reboot. If you see the box in Figure 2-2, press the Enter key to choose Restart Windows.

FIGURE 2-2. *The choices you may see at the end of Windows Setup if you are reinstalling Windows.*

Now that Windows is set up, you're ready for Chapter 3, "Starting Out, Finding Your Way, and Quitting."

Chapter 3

Starting Out, Finding Your Way, and Quitting

Starting the Windows operating system is simple. Look at your computer screen, and you'll see something called the MS-DOS prompt (usually a letter and a greater-than symbol, such as *C*>). Now use the keyboard to type the word *win*, and press the Enter key. That's it! (It takes a few seconds for your computer to start Windows, so don't be alarmed if the copyright notice flashes and disappears and your computer screen looks blank for a bit.)

The very first time you start Windows you see the Program Manager window as shown in Figure 3-1 on the following page. Program Manager is your home base in Windows—the first thing you see when you start Windows (unless you make modifications) and the last thing you see when you quit. In between these two times, you return to Program Manager whenever you need to start another application.

This chapter describes opening, switching, and closing the windows inside Program Manager (called *group windows*). The group windows contain little pictures (called *icons*) for the applications in your computer, and the chapter goes on to describe how to start, switch, and quit applications. After a description of how to quit Windows, the chapter ends with a summary of all this important "navigational" information in a section called "Finding Your Way Home."

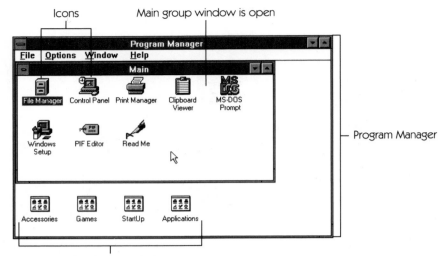

FIGURE 3-1. *The initial appearance of Program Manager.*

If Windows Looks Different from Figure 3-1

If Windows was previously installed on your computer, and someone has already been using it, you might see something very different from Figure 3-1. You might see something very confusing. One of the advantages of Windows is that you can open many applications and modify their arrangement to suit yourself. Well, the downside of this accessibility of information and flexibility of design is that you can have lots of images on the screen in Windows. These images may overlap one another. Even if the images aren't overlapping one another, you might find the quantity of information confusing, particularly as someone new to Windows.

And you might create a profusion of overlapping images yourself by clicking lots of icons and buttons. It's a pretty natural thing to do as you first learn and explore Windows.

If you want to simplify your Windows view, go directly to the section below called "Minimizing Group Windows" and the section called "Quitting Applications." This is your safety net when things get confusing in Windows—minimizing some of the windows and quitting some of the applications that clutter your computer screen.

THE GROUP WINDOWS
INSIDE PROGRAM MANAGER

Program Manager is different from most applications because it has windows inside of it called group windows. These windows may be *open* or *minimized*. Figure 3-1 shows Program Manager with one group window open and the rest minimized. The open group window is called Main; you can tell because its name is written in the *title bar* at the top of the window.

Inside the Main group window you'll see icons with titles underneath that give the names of various applications. All of the applications grouped together in Main are similar in that they handle basic tasks of the Windows operating system—like finding and changing work files (File Manager) and changing the way Windows looks (Control Panel).

This is what group windows are for, grouping together similar applications. The Accessories group window contains applications like Calendar, Calculator, and Clock. The Games group window contains games called Minesweeper and Solitaire.

When you start Windows for the first time, only one of the group windows in Program Manager is opened, but they all could be opened, arranged in various ways, or all minimized. In other words, there are any number of ways that the appearance of Program Manager could change. In fact, it's easy to have group windows completely covering other group windows in Program Manager. If you ever get confused, you can always simplify the image in front of you by minimizing any group windows that are open.

Opening Group Windows

You can open a minimized group window by *double-clicking* it with the mouse. (If you don't have a mouse, read the Tip at the end of this chapter called "If You Don't Have a Mouse.") To open a minimized group window, first move the mouse on your desk. You'll notice that an arrow moves on your screen. The arrow is called the *mouse pointer*. By moving the mouse on your desk, position the mouse pointer on the screen so that its point is over the minimized group window called Games, as in Figure 3-2.

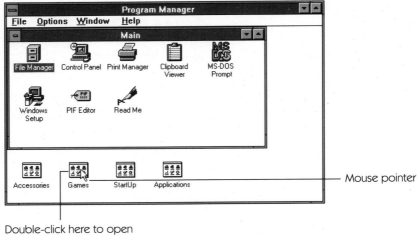

— Mouse pointer

Double-click here to open
the Games group window

FIGURE 3-2. *The mouse pointer positioned over a minimized group window.*

Now hold the mouse steady. Notice that there are two buttons on the mouse. While continuing to hold the mouse steady, press the left button quickly twice. This is called a double-click. The Games window should open as in Figure 3-3. If the window didn't open, one of two things probably went wrong: either the point of the mouse pointer wasn't over the minimized group window, or you didn't press the mouse button quickly enough. Try again.

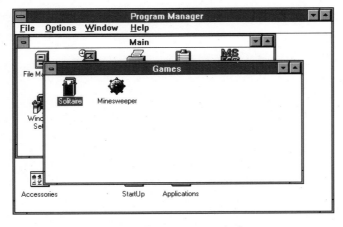

FIGURE 3-3. *The opened Games group window.*

Here's a second method you can use to open a minimized group window, if you had trouble double-clicking. Position the mouse cursor over the minimized group window again. This time, press the left mouse button just once. This is called *clicking*. The title of the minimized group window will be highlighted. (There will be color behind the letters.) You will also see a *menu* above the minimized window. A menu is a list of *commands* that you can click to initiate an action. The menu that appears above the Minimized group window is called the *Control Menu*, and when it opens, the Restore command is highlighted. See Figure 3-4. If you now press the Enter key on your keyboard, the group window will open.

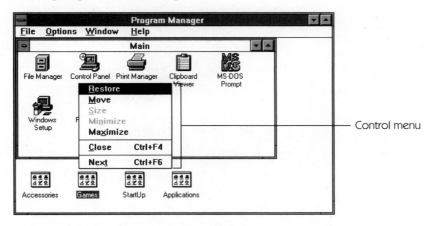

FIGURE 3-4. *The minimized Games group window with an open Control menu.*

Switching Between Group Windows

In Figure 3-3 you'll notice that the Games group window is in front of Main. The title bar of Games is filled with color and the title bar of Main isn't. If you want to see the Main window you need to "bring it to the front" by making it the *active* window. There are a couple of easy ways to accomplish this. First, when any part of the Main group window is visible behind Games, as it is in this case, you can click anywhere in it with the mouse, as shown in Figure 3-5. You'll see the Main window move to the front as in Figure 3-6. Main now has a colored title bar, and is the active window.

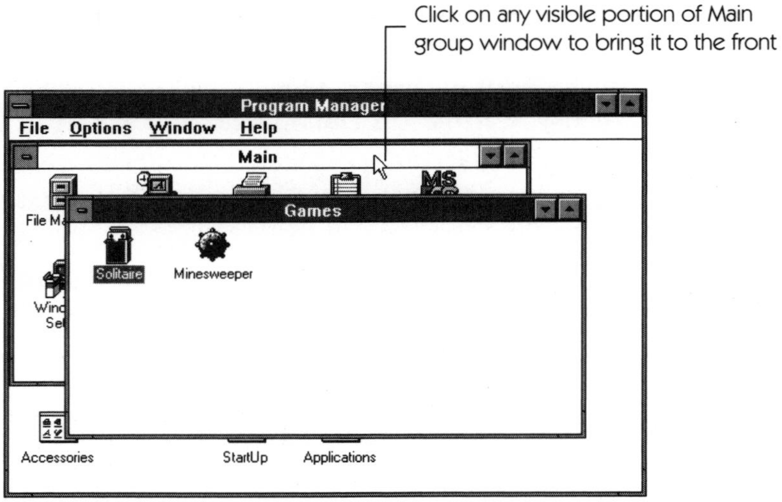

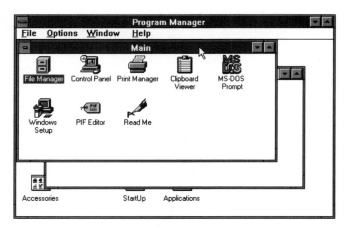

Click on any visible portion of Main group window to bring it to the front

FIGURE 3-5. *Switching group windows by clicking with the mouse.*

FIGURE 3-6. *The Main group window after switching to it (making it the active window).*

Another way to switch between group windows is to use two keys on the keyboard. They are used together in what is called a *key combination*. Find the Ctrl key and press it. Then, while keeping the Ctrl key pressed down, press the Tab key. (This and other key combinations are expressed in this book by writing the key names with a + sign between them, as in Ctrl+Tab.) Keep the

Ctrl key held down, and then press the Tab key again and again. You'll see that this not only switches between the open group windows but between all the group windows, including the minimized ones.

Minimizing Group Windows

Knowing how to minimize a group window in Program Manager can be very helpful when you're learning about Windows. It's a way to simplify the images on the screen in front of you. To minimize an open group window, you can double-click in the box that contains a horizontal line in the upper left corner of the open window, as shown in Figure 3-7. The box is called the *Control-menu box.*

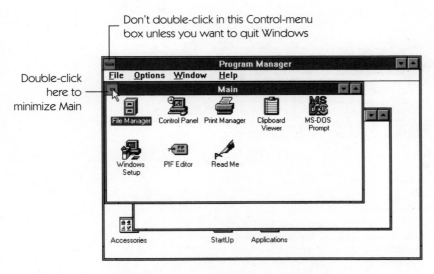

FIGURE 3-7. *Minimizing the Main group window.*

NOTE *If you double-click in the Control-menu box in the Program Manager window, you will quit Program Manager. See Figure 3-7. Quitting Program Manager is the way you quit Windows! If you do try to quit Windows, a little box will pop up that says* This will end your Windows session. *The box has two buttons in it that say* OK *and* Cancel. *If you click the Cancel button you will not quit Windows.*

To double-click in the Control-menu box, move the mouse so that the mouse pointer (the arrow on the screen) moves. Position the mouse pointer so that its point is over the Control-menu box. Now hold the mouse steady and press the left mouse button quickly twice. If the group window didn't minimize, one of two things probably went wrong: either the point of the mouse pointer wasn't over the box, or you didn't press the mouse button quickly enough. Try again.

There's another way to minimize a group window that you might find a little easier. Click once in the Control-menu box. The Control menu will open as shown in Figure 3-8. Click the command that says *Close* and the group window will close.

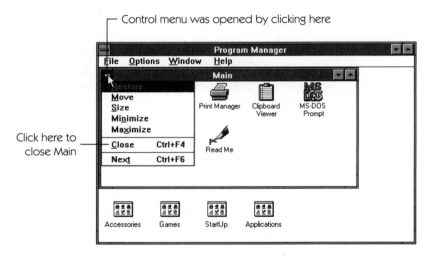

FIGURE 3-8. *Using the Control menu to close a group window.*

APPLICATIONS

The group windows in Program Manager contain the icons for your applications. (There is an Applications group window that contains icons for all of the applications that you buy and install separately from Windows, but don't get confused. All the group windows have applications in them.) Just about anything you want to do in Windows is begun by starting an application. Thanks to Windows the process of starting an application is very simple. It's also simple to start several applications, to have them all running at the same time, and to switch between them. Finally, you can quit applications easily. When you're learning Windows you can quit applications to simplify the proliferation of windows on your computer screen.

Starting Applications

Right now, open the Games group window in Program Manager if it isn't already open. Use whatever techniques you need from those described above (for opening a group window, switching between group windows, or minimizing a group window). The open Games group window is shown in Figure 3-9.

Start the Minesweeper game by double-clicking the Minesweeper icon. (If you don't have a mouse, read the tip at the end of this chapter called "If You Don't Have a Mouse.") To double-click, move the mouse so that the mouse pointer (the arrow on the screen) moves. Position the mouse pointer so that its point is over the icon. See Figure 3-9. Now hold the mouse steady and press the left mouse button quickly twice. You should see the game as shown in Figure 3-10. If the game didn't start, one of two things probably went wrong: either the point of the mouse pointer wasn't over the icon, or you didn't press the mouse button quickly enough. Try again.

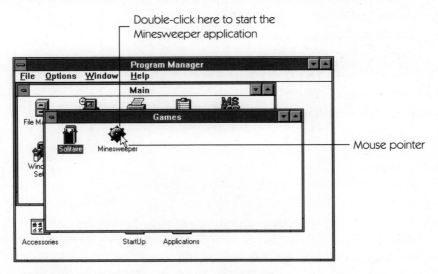

FIGURE 3-9. *The mouse pointer over an application icon.*

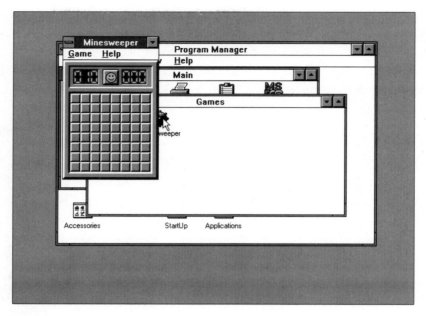

FIGURE 3-10. *The Minesweeper game.*

Here's another way to start an application: Click (not double-click) the application icon with the mouse. The application title should then be highlighted. Press the Enter key to start the application.

Switching Between Applications

One of the benefits of Windows is that you can run several applications simultaneously. You can start a drawing application like Paintbrush and create a picture, and then you can switch to Program Manager and start a word processing application like Write so that you can write a report. At any time you can switch back to Paintbrush so that you can copy your picture for inclusion in your report. (In Chapter 24 you'll find out how to copy a picture into Write.) And at any time you can switch back to Program Manager to start Calculator or Calendar or any other application as well.

To practice switching between applications, make sure that you have started Minesweeper. (See "Starting Applications" above.) When you start Minesweeper it partly covers Program Manager, as shown in Figure 3-10.

You'll notice also that Minesweeper's title bar is colored and Program Manager's isn't. Suppose you wanted to make the Program Manager window the active window and "bring it to the front." One way to switch from Minesweeper to Program Manager is to click in any visible portion of Program Manager. Now Minesweeper should be "in back of" Program Manager, as in Figure 3-11. You can just barely see the top of the Minesweeper window behind Program Manager. To bring Minesweeper to the front again, click in any visible portion of its window.

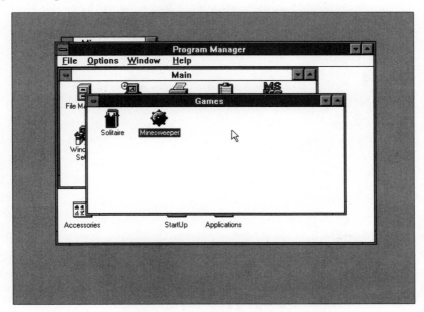

FIGURE 3-11. *Program Manager after switching to it (making it the active window).*

Sometimes an application you start will be very large on the screen, completely covering any other applications you also have running, including Program Manager. Then you'll need to use some keys from the keyboard, pressing them at the same time in a key combination, to switch between applications. Press the Alt key and hold it down while you press and release the Tab key. See what happens. A little box appears on your screen with the name of another running application, as shown in Figure 3-12. If you continue holding down the Alt key while you repeatedly press and release the Tab key you'll see a repeating series of boxes with the names of all your running applications. Try it. When you see a box with the name of an application you want to switch to, release the Alt key; Windows will bring that application to the front.

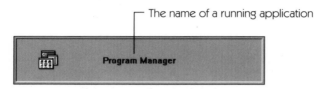

The name of a running application

FIGURE 3-12. *A box appears when you switch applications with Alt+Tab.*

NOTE *If you press Alt+Tab but release the Alt key between presses of the Tab key, you will switch between the last two applications you used. This is a handy technique to use when you're mainly working in two applications. But if you want to cycle through* all *of the applications you have running, you must keep the Alt key held down between presses of the Tab key.*

Quitting Applications

Knowing how to quit an application can be very helpful to you as you're learning about Windows. It's a way to simplify the images on the screen in front of you. To quit an application you can use the same procedure you used to minimize an open group window. Double-click in the Control-menu box, the box that contains a horizontal line, in the upper left corner of the application window, as shown in Figure 3-13.

Double-click here to
quit Minesweeper

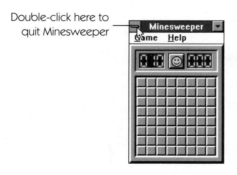

FIGURE 3-13. *Quitting the Minesweeper application.*

NOTE *If you double-click in the Control-menu box in the Program Manager window, you will quit Program Manager. See Figure 3-7. Quitting Program Manager is the way you quit Windows! If you do try to quit Windows, a little box will pop up that says* This will end your Windows session. *The box has two buttons in it that are labeled* OK *and* Cancel. *If you click the Cancel button, you will not quit Windows.*

To double-click in the Control-menu box, move the mouse so that the mouse pointer (the arrow on the screen) moves. Position the mouse pointer so that its point is over the Control-menu box. Now hold the mouse steady and press the left mouse button quickly twice. If the application window doesn't disappear from the screen, one of two things probably went wrong: either the point of the mouse pointer wasn't over the Control-menu box, or you didn't press the mouse button quickly enough. Try again.

There's another way to quit an application that you might find a little easier. Click in the Control-menu box. The Control menu will open as shown in Figure 3-14. Click the command that says *Close* and the window will close. That is, the application will quit running and the application's window will disappear from the screen.

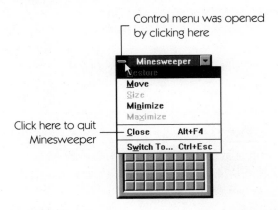

FIGURE 3-14. *Using the Control menu to quit an application.*

QUITTING WINDOWS

To quit Windows you must first return to Program Manager. You can then double-click in the Control-menu box in the upper left corner of the Program Manager window. You can also quit by first clicking in the Control-menu box to open the Control menu and then clicking the Close command. These procedures are explained in more detail in the previous sections called "Minimizing Group Windows" and "Quitting Applications." When you have successfully given Program Manager the command to close, the box shown in Figure 3-15 will pop up on your screen. Click the OK button to quit Windows, or click the Cancel button to return to Windows without quitting.

FIGURE 3-15. *The Exit Windows message box.*

FINDING YOUR WAY HOME

This chapter has described the procedures for starting and quitting Windows. It has also told you how to open, switch, and minimize group windows in Program Manager and how to start, switch, and quit applications. With these basic actions you'll always be able to find your way around Windows and back home again. These actions are summarized in Figures 3-16, 3-17, and 3-18 below.

Windows Basics	What You Do
Starting Windows	At the *C>* prompt, type *win* and then press the Enter key
Quitting Windows	Double-click in the Control-menu box (box with a horizontal line in upper left corner of Program Manager)

FIGURE 3-16. *The procedures for starting and quitting Windows.*

Program Manager Basics	What You Do
Opening a group window	Double-click minimized group window
Switching between group windows	Press Ctrl+Tab (press and hold the Ctrl key while pressing Tab repeatedly)
Minimizing a group window	Double-click in the Control-menu box (box with a horizontal line in upper left corner of group window)

FIGURE 3-17. *The procedures for opening, switching, and minimizing group windows in Program Manager.*

Applications Basics	What You Do
Starting an application	Double-click an application's icon inside a group window
Switching between applications	Press Alt+Tab (press and hold the Alt key while pressing Tab repeatedly, then release Alt)
Quitting an application	Double-click in Control-menu box (box with a horizontal line in upper left corner of application window)

FIGURE 3-18. *The procedures for opening, switching, and quitting applications.*

If You Don't Have a Mouse

If you don't have a mouse, there are keyboard actions you can take to control group windows in Program Manager. To open a group window in Program Manager, press the Ctrl+Tab key combination (press and hold the Ctrl key while you repeatedly press Tab) until the minimized group window you want to open has a highlighted title. Then press the Enter key. Ctrl+Tab will switch you between open group windows as well as minimized ones. To close a group window, switch to the group window and press Ctrl+F4 (press and hold the Ctrl key while you press the key labeled F4 *on the left or top of your keyboard).*

If you don't have a mouse, there are keyboard actions you can take to control applications. To start an application, open the group window that contains the application's icon (using the Ctrl+Tab key combination and the Enter key). Use the arrow keys on your keyboard until the title of the application you want to open is highlighted, and then press Enter. To switch between running applications, use the Alt+Tab key combination (press and hold the Alt key while you repeatedly press Tab), and then release Alt when you see the name (inside a box on the screen) of the application you want to switch to. To quit an application with the keyboard, switch to the application and press Alt+F4 (press and hold the Alt key while you press the key labeled F4 *on the left or top of your keyboard).*

Chapter 4

Using the Mouse

The mouse has been described as "that thing that looks like a bar of soap with a wire attached." It's a very useful device. For many actions you want to take in the Windows operating system, the mouse gives you the easiest way.

In Chapter 3 you learned how to use the mouse to find your way around in Windows by opening, switching, and minimizing group windows in Program Manager and by starting, switching, and quitting applications. In this chapter we'll describe some mouse basics and then give you lots of opportunities to practice mouse skills by showing you the Minesweeper game application.

MOUSE BASICS

Any action you take with the mouse has two steps. First, you move the mouse on your desk to move a pointer on your computer screen. Second, you use the buttons on the mouse to initiate the action.

Positioning the Mouse and Moving the Pointer

Figure 4-1 shows you how most people hold and position the mouse while they work. You move the mouse on your desk, and an arrow moves on the computer screen. If you're not familiar with a mouse, try it. Move the mouse, and watch the arrow on the screen move. This arrow is called the *mouse pointer* or simply the *pointer*. When you are comfortable with moving the mouse to move the pointer, lift the mouse off the desk. Notice that the pointer doesn't move when you lift the mouse. Set the mouse down at a different spot on the desk. Now move the mouse again. You use this "lift and set down" technique when you run out of desk space but still need to move the pointer farther.

FIGURE 4-1. *The position of the mouse while you work.*

Using Mouse Buttons

Most mouse models attached to IBM and compatible computers have either two buttons or three buttons. Windows uses two buttons—the left button and the right button. Usually, the left button is set up as the primary button; that means you will use the left button most of the time. The right button is usually set up as the secondary button; that means you will use the right button only occasionally, for special purposes. Less frequently still, you'll need to press both the left and right mouse buttons at the same time.

If you want to change which mouse buttons are the primary and secondary ones (maybe because you prefer to manipulate the mouse with your left hand), see the section "Controlling the Mouse," in Chapter 15.

Now you're ready to really use the mouse. To be a great mouser, learn how to *click*, *drag*, and *double-click*.

Clicking

Clicking means pressing and releasing the mouse button without moving the mouse.

Dragging

Dragging means holding down the mouse button and, while you're holding down the mouse button, moving the mouse. You use this action to move windows and icons around the screen and sometimes to highlight an area of the screen.

Double-clicking

Double-clicking is a repeated click without moving the mouse: press–release–press–release. If you move the mouse between clicks, even a little bit, Windows thinks you did two separate clicks. So when you double-click, be sure to hold the mouse absolutely still. You can change the speed of double-clicking so that Windows allows more or less time between the two clicks. If you want to change the double-click speed, see the section "Controlling the Mouse," in Chapter 15.

Going Back to the Windows Tutorial

Windows includes a tutorial that demonstrates the basics of using the mouse. The Windows Setup program even asks you during installation whether you want to run the Windows Tutorial. Perhaps you missed or passed on that opportunity. If so (or if you just want to take the tutorial again), you can start the Windows Tutorial from Program Manager.

To run the Windows Tutorial, first switch to Program Manager if you're not already there by clicking its window or by pressing Alt+Tab. Next open the Help menu by clicking the word Help *near the top of the Program Manager window (see the picture below). Finally you click the Windows Tutorial command.*

After the Windows Tutorial window appears on your screen, follow the directions that are given. When you finish the Windows Tutorial, Windows returns you to Program Manager.

GETTING READY TO PLAY MINESWEEPER

Minesweeper is one of the games included with Windows. The purpose of the games is to give you practice using the mouse. (At least, that's what you can tell anyone who sees you hard at play!) The real purpose is to have some fun. So let's have some fun.

In the game of Minesweeper, the game board is made up of "covered" squares. Some of the squares contain hidden mines. The object of the game is to uncover all the squares that don't contain mines. If you uncover a mine, you are "killed" and so lose the game. You use the mouse to uncover all the safe squares and to make other moves that can help you win the game.

Starting the Game

To start the game of Minesweeper, return to Program Manager (if you're not already there) by clicking in the Program Manager window or by pressing Alt+Tab. In Program Manager, use Ctrl+Tab to switch to the Games group window, which is either open or minimized. If the Games group window is minimized, press Enter to open it. The open Games group window is shown in Figure 4-2. Now start the Minesweeper game by double-clicking the Minesweeper icon. The game board is shown in Figure 4-3.

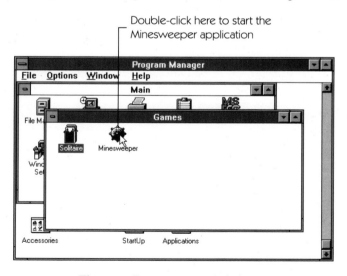

FIGURE 4-2. *The open Games group window.*

FIGURE 4-3. *The Minesweeper window.*

 Minesweeper, like all applications for Windows, contains help at your fingertips. You can press F1 or use the Help menu to display Help.

To use the Help menu, click the word **Help**, *which is just below the name* Minesweeper *at the top of the application. This step will open the Help menu. Then click the Contents command.*

When the Help window appears, you can display and read additional Help information. This procedure is described in detail in Chapter 9. You can leave the Help window on display while you play the game so that you can easily get more help. Use Alt+Tab to switch between the Help window and the Minesweeper game window at any time.

To quit the Help application (in other words, to close the Help window until you need it again), double-click the Control-menu box.

Double-click here to close the Minesweeper Help window

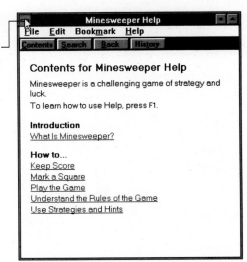

Using the Title Bar to Position the Game Board

When you start Minesweeper, its window (the game board) appears in the upper left corner of your screen. You might prefer to center the game board on the screen. To center the window, drag it to the middle of the screen. To drag a window, move the mouse until the mouse pointer is on the title bar (located at the top of the window), hold down the left mouse button, move the mouse until the window is where you want it, and then release the mouse button. While you drag the window you'll see a gray outline of the window's new position.

You can drag any window that has not been *maximized* (enlarged to fill the entire screen). Maximizing is explained in Chapter 6, "Sizing and Moving a Window."

LET'S GO A COUPLE OF ROUNDS

Now that you see the game board and know some mouse techniques, click squares to uncover what's under them. That is, move the mouse until the pointer is on a square, and then press and release the left mouse button. A square contains either a mine, a number, or a blank. (Notice the happy face at the top of the game board as you click the mouse button.)

One strategy you can use to start a game is to click the square in each corner of the game board. You'll find that Minesweeper automatically exposes some unmined areas.

FIGURE 4-4. *The Minesweeper game board with the squares in the four corners clicked.*

Now you can start to analyze the game. A number in a square tells you how many mines are hidden within the eight squares that surround that square. If the number is 1, only one of the eight surrounding squares contains a mine. For example, in Figure 4-4, the 1 nearest the lower left corner shows you that the square off its right shoulder contains a mine because all the other adjacent squares are uncovered and don't contain a mine. (Remember, you can press F1 to get more detailed game instructions.)

In Minesweeper you can use the secondary (usually the one on the right) mouse button and both mouse buttons together to help you win a game. When you have figured out that a square contains a mine, point to that square and click the secondary mouse button. Minesweeper displays a flag on that square to indicate that you believe the square contains a mine. See Figure 4-5. As long as a square displays a flag, you can't click the square to uncover it, accidentally blowing yourself up.

FIGURE 4-5. *Setting a flag to mark a mine.*

If you do get blown up, the game board will show all the mines, the happy face will stop looking happy, and you won't be able to do a thing. Figure 4-6 shows the grim aftermath. The only thing you can do after hitting a mine is to start a new game by clicking the face at the top center of the window.

Click here to start
a new game

FIGURE 4-6. *An example of the Minesweeper game after you hit a mine.*

When you are playing and have all the mines in an area marked, you can use the mouse another way: clicking both mouse buttons to uncover the surrounding squares. For example, you can point to the 1 to the left of the flag in Figure 4-5 and click both buttons at the same time. As long as you have the mines flagged correctly in the eight surrounding squares, Minesweeper uncovers the rest of the adjacent squares, as in Figure 4-7. If you haven't yet marked the correct number of mines, nothing happens. If you have marked the correct *number* of mines but marked them on the *wrong squares*, Minesweeper uncovers a mine when you use a two-button click and KABLOOHEY! You're mincemeat.

FIGURE 4-7. *Clicking both buttons uncovers surrounding squares.*

If you uncover all the numbered and blank squares without uncovering a mine, you are cool, as the happy face shows you. Also, if you won the game in record time, Minesweeper asks for your name. (See Figure 4-8.)

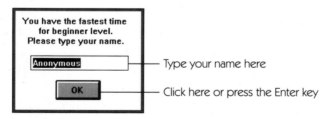

FIGURE 4-8. *The Minesweeper fastest time dialog box.*

Minesweeper then shows a little window (called a *dialog box*) that displays the fastest time for each level of play and the name of the player who got that time. (See Figure 4-9.)

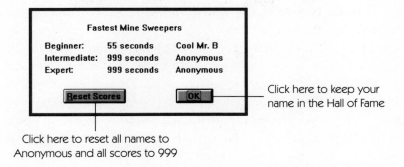

Fastest Mine Sweepers

Beginner:	55 seconds	Cool Mr. B
Intermediate:	999 seconds	Anonymous
Expert:	999 seconds	Anonymous

Reset Scores   OK

Click here to keep your
name in the Hall of Fame

Click here to reset all names to
Anonymous and all scores to 999

FIGURE 4-9. *The Fastest Mine Sweepers dialog box.*

If you haven't won a game in record time, you won't be asked for your name! But in Chapter 5 you'll learn how to bring up the Fastest Mine Sweepers dialog box on your own. You'll also try playing Minesweeper at a higher level of difficulty, and at the same time learn a few things about menus, commands, and dialog boxes.

Chapter 5

Using Menus, Commands, and Dialog Boxes

In the last chapter you practiced your mouse skills by playing a few games of Minesweeper. You won a few games and set some records. Now that you've played at the Beginner level for a while, you're probably ready for a bigger challenge. Minesweeper provides two more built-in levels of difficulty, and the opportunity to create your own custom game. To make these changes you use menus, commands, and dialog boxes.

At the top of the window in most applications for the Windows operating system, you see the *menu bar*. The Minesweeper menu bar is pointed out in Figure 5-1.

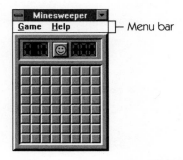 — Menu bar

FIGURE 5-1. *The Minesweeper menu bar.*

Each name on the menu bar is the title of a menu. As you'll soon see, each menu contains a list of actions you can take, called commands. The following sections explain how to open and close a menu and how to choose a command from a menu. You'll also gain a little more experience with dialog boxes.

OPENING A MENU

To open a menu, you click its name. If you prefer to use the keyboard, press the Alt key and then press the letter key that matches the underlined letter in the menu's name. The menu appears below the menu's name. Try opening the Game menu. Figure 5-2 shows what it looks like.

FIGURE 5-2. *The opened Game menu in Minesweeper.*

CLOSING A MENU

If you want to close a menu without doing anything, click anywhere outside the menu. (Be careful you don't accidentally click something else that causes an action!) Or, with the keyboard, press the Alt key. The menu will close but the menu name will remain highlighted. Press the Alt key again to remove the highlight.

CHOOSING COMMANDS

Now you're ready to make some things happen. Here's where you practice choosing commands.

Choosing the Best Times Command

In Chapter 4 you learned that the Fastest Mine Sweepers dialog box appears automatically on your screen when you win a Minesweeper game in record time. You can look at this dialog box whenever you want by opening the

Game menu and clicking the Best Times command. (See Figure 5-2.) Notice that the Best Times command on the Game menu has three dots after its name. These dots mean that the command will always bring up a dialog box. Click the Best Times command now. The dialog box, shown in Figure 5-3, will appear on your screen.

FIGURE 5-3. *The Fastest Mine Sweepers dialog box.*

When you're done with a dialog box, you can make it go away by clicking a button, usually the OK button. Many dialog boxes also have a Cancel button. When you click the OK button, you tell the application to close the dialog box and to *accept any changes* you made in the dialog box. (If the OK button has a heavy outline around it, you can also press Enter to close the dialog box and accept changes.) If a dialog box has a Cancel button, you can click Cancel to close the dialog box *without accepting any changes* you made. (Pressing the Esc key will do the same thing as clicking Cancel.) Click OK in the Fastest Mine Sweepers dialog box now to make it go away.

There is another way to open a menu and choose a command, and it takes only one step. You might want to try it now to open the Fastest Mine Sweepers dialog box again. You drag from the menu name down the open menu and release the mouse button at the command you want. In other words, move the mouse pointer over the menu name, and press the primary (usually the left) mouse button and hold it. As you move the mouse downward through the menu, you'll see that the command under the mouse pointer is highlighted. Release the mouse button when the mouse pointer is over the Best Times command. You will see the Fastest Mine Sweepers dialog box again. Click OK to close the dialog box.

A third way to choose a command is to use only the keyboard. You learned how to open a menu by pressing Alt, releasing it, and then pressing the underlined letter in the menu's name. (For example, you can open the

Game menu by pressing Alt and then G.) With the menu open, you can use the keyboard to choose a command by pressing the key of the underlined letter in the command name. In the Best Times command, the underlined letter is T. Try this, and then click OK to close the dialog box.

Choosing a Skill-Level Command

You can change the level of difficulty in the game by choosing other commands. The Game menu lets you choose one of three built-in skill levels: Beginner, Intermediate, and Expert. The levels have different numbers of squares and different numbers of mines, as shown in Figure 5-4.

Skill Level	Number of Squares	Number of Mines
Beginner	64 (8x8)	10
Intermediate	256 (16x16)	40
Expert	480 (16x30)	99

FIGURE 5-4. *The number of squares and mines for each skill level in Minesweeper.*

To change the skill level of the game, open the Game menu by clicking Game (or by pressing Alt and then G), and then choose the skill level by clicking the command for the skill level you want (or by pressing B for Beginner, I for Intermediate, or E for Expert). These commands do not have dots after their names on the menu because there are no dialog boxes associated with the commands. Notice that after you choose a skill-level command, the menu closes and Minesweeper performs the action. In this case, Minesweeper sets up a new game at the skill level you chose.

MINIMIZING AND RESTORING YOUR GAME

To round out your current knowledge of Windows, you need to understand some basic ways to change the size of an application window. Suppose you want to put an application ''aside''—to get it out of the way, yet have it easily accessible to use later. You can *minimize* its window, which means to turn it into an icon.

In the upper right corner of the Minesweeper window, you see a triangle pointing downward, as shown in Figure 5-5. The button that contains this triangle is called the *Minimize button.*

FIGURE 5-5. *The Minimize button.*

Try clicking this button with the mouse. (If you don't have a mouse, see the Tip at the end of this chapter.) You turn the Minesweeper window into an icon, and, depending on how your other windows are arranged, it may disappear from view. If you can't see it, rest assured that the icon is on the screen. It is probably hidden by another window. The icon is shown in Figure 5-6.

FIGURE 5-6. *The Minesweeper icon (minimized window).*

When you want to restore the Minesweeper window to its usual size, you can use a method you've already learned: Cycle through your running applications with Alt+Tab. When the name *Minesweeper* appears in the box in the center of the screen, release the Alt key. The Minesweeper game board will then be restored to its previous size.

If the icon isn't hidden, other options are available to you to restore your Minesweeper game. The easiest way is to double-click the Minesweeper icon.

MAKING CHANGES IN DIALOG BOXES

Sometimes Windows displays a dialog box that contains choices for you to select or spaces for you to fill in. These dialog boxes look something like an order form in a merchandise catalog.

The Custom Field dialog box in Minesweeper allows you to set up a custom game that contains more or fewer mines than are contained in the preset skill levels. Also, you can set the number of squares in the game. To open the Custom Field dialog box, first click the Game menu to open it and then click the Custom command. Figure 5-7 shows you the dialog box that appears.

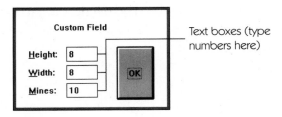

FIGURE 5-7. *The Custom Field dialog box.*

In the Custom Field dialog box, the three boxes that contain numbers are called *text boxes*. A text box is a rectangle in which you type information. Note that in the text boxes in this dialog box you can type only numbers. Other characters appear if you type them, but Minesweeper ignores them. In other text boxes in Windows, you can type only letters of the alphabet.

Suppose you want to set up a custom game that is 10 squares high and 10 squares wide and contains 30 mines. All you have to do is fill in the text boxes, as shown in Figure 5-8, and then click the OK button or press the Enter key. But how do you fill in the text boxes? There are several ways, two that use the mouse and one that uses the keyboard.

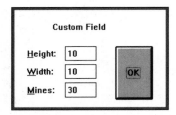

FIGURE 5-8. *The Custom Field dialog box for a 10x10 game with 30 mines.*

Filling in Text Boxes by Clicking and Editing

One way to change the value in a text box is by clicking and editing. (If you prefer to use a keyboard, see ''Using the Keyboard'' below.) To change the value in the Height text box from 8 to 10, you first move the mouse so that its pointer is over the text box. Notice that the pointer changes shape from an arrow to an I-beam. But you can't type yet! The I-beam helps you get to the right spot for typing. Move the I-beam so that it's just to the right of the 8 in the text box. Now click the mouse button. A blinking vertical line, called the *insertion point,* appears immediately to the right of the 8 in the text box. It marks the spot at which text you type will appear. If you typed *10* now, the value in the text box would be *810.* To fill in the text box with the number 10, you first have to press the Backspace key once to erase the 8. Now type *10.* Simple, right? An even simpler way to replace values in text boxes is the "double-click and replace" method.

Filling in Text Boxes by Double-Clicking and Replacing

Try double-clicking anywhere in a text box. (If you prefer to use a keyboard, see "Using the Keyboard" below.) You'll notice that the number in that box is highlighted (has a colored square behind it). If you start typing a new number, it will replace the number in the square. If you decide you don't want to replace the number after you've highlighted it, click once in the text box. This will take you into the editing mode that was described above.

Using the Keyboard

If you prefer the keyboard, you have to use one of several techniques for moving between the text boxes. First, you can use the Alt key in a key combination with the underlined letter in the text box name. For example, in the Custom Field dialog box, you can press Alt+W to move to the Width text box. Again, a key combination means you press the Alt key and hold it down while you press W. Another way to move to different elements in a dialog box is by pressing the Tab key.

With these keyboard techniques, when you move to a text box, the number in the box is highlighted. You then start typing a new number, and the new number will replace the old.

When you've entered the new numbers, click the OK button or press Enter. The custom game is ready.

After you set up a custom game, you play the game in the same way you play the games with preset skill levels. Minesweeper doesn't, however, keep a record of best scores for custom games.

NOTE *Up to this point in the book, directions have been fairly explicit about how to open menus, choose commands, go to text boxes, and choose buttons. To simplify things, the rest of the book will use standard descriptions for some actions. Figure 5-9 summarizes these descriptions.*

Standard Description	What You Do
Choose the Custom command from the Game menu (Alt,G,C).	Open the Game menu, either by clicking its menu name or by pressing the Alt key and then the G key. Choose the Custom command, either by clicking its name or by pressing the C key.
Go to the Height text box.	Click or double-click in the Height text box; or press the Tab key repeatedly until the Height text box is highlighted.
Choose OK.	Click the OK button, or (if the OK button has a heavy outline) press the Enter key.
Choose Cancel.	Click the Cancel button, or press the Esc key.

FIGURE 5-9. *Examples of standard descriptions for actions you take involving menus, commands, text boxes, and buttons.*

QUITTING THE GAME

To quit Minesweeper, use the technique you learned in Chapter 3, ''Starting Out, Finding Your Way, and Quitting'': Double-click in the Control-menu box in the upper left corner of the window.

If You Don't Have a Mouse

To minimize and restore windows when you don't have a mouse, use the Control menu. (First, make sure the window you want to change is active. If not, use Alt+Tab.) Press the Alt key and then press the spacebar. This will open the application's Control menu whether the application's window is minimized or normal size. The Control menu is used like other menus. When the Control menu is open, you can press the N key to minimize an application window that is open. You can press the R key to "restore" to normal size an application window that is minimized.

For keyboard users, two techniques were discussed in this chapter for moving to a text box (or other element) inside a dialog box. You can press Alt, hold it down, and press the key of the underlined letter in the text box name. You can also press the Tab key to move from element to element.

To quit an application when you don't have a mouse, press Alt+F4. (Press the Alt key and hold it down while you press the key labeled F4 at the left or top of your keyboard.)

Chapter 6

Sizing and Moving a Window

In this chapter you'll learn about sizing and moving a window. You'll work with Paintbrush, the drawing application that comes with the Windows operating system. Operations like sizing and moving should give you a sense of how really cool Windows is. You can directly manipulate objects that you see on the screen, and do it in an easy, natural way with the mouse. For this reason, use of the mouse is emphasized in the pages that follow. (If you need or want to use the keyboard, be sure to read the Tip ''If You Don't Have a Mouse,'' at the end of this chapter.)

When you've learned about sizing and moving a window, you can slide into Chapter 7, where you'll have fun drawing in Paintbrush and learn a little about working in an application.

MOUSE PAINTING

Windows includes a drawing application named Paintbrush that gives you the means to create your own pictures in color or in black and white. Start Paintbrush now from the Accessories group window of Program Manager. Here's a review of the steps you need to take to start Paintbrush, as explained in Chapter 3, ''Starting Out, Finding Your Way, and Quitting'':

1. Switch to Program Manager by clicking in its window or, if necessary, by pressing Alt+Tab.

2. Switch to the Accessories group window by clicking in it or, if it isn't visible, by pressing Ctrl+Tab.

3. Open the Accessories group window, if it's minimized, by double-clicking it (Figure 6-1).

4. Find the Paintbrush icon, if it's not visible, by pressing the letter P.

5. Start the Paintbrush application by double-clicking its icon (Figure 6-2).

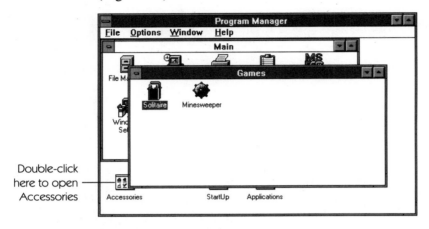

Double-click here to open Accessories

FIGURE 6-1. *The Program Manager window with the Accessories group window minimized.*

Double-click here to start Paintbrush

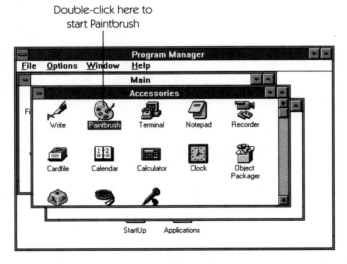

FIGURE 6-2. *The Accessories group window contains Paintbrush.*

After Windows starts Paintbrush, you see the Paintbrush window on your screen, as shown in Figure 6-3.

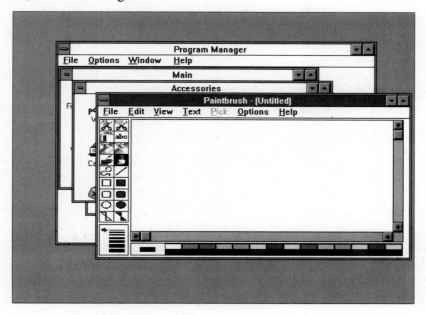

FIGURE 6-3. *The Paintbrush window.*

MAXIMIZING

When Paintbrush starts, the window doesn't take up the entire screen. To *maximize* the window so that it fills the screen, you click the Maximize button in the upper right corner of the title bar, as shown in Figure 6-4.

FIGURE 6-4. *The Paintbrush title bar with the Maximize button in the right corner.*

Try maximizing the Paintbrush window. Not only does the window get larger but there is a change in the title bar. The Restore button replaces the Maximize button on the title bar, as shown in Figure 6-5. When a window is maximized, clicking the Restore button returns the window to the size it was before you maximized it.

Click here to restore
the window

FIGURE 6-5. *The Restore button replaces the Maximize button on the title bar.*

Try restoring your Paintbrush window. The Maximize button again appears at the right end of the title bar.

SIZING

You already know about maximizing, restoring, and minimizing windows. Now you can learn about changing the size of a restored window by moving its borders. (Remember that you can't move the borders of a maximized or minimized window—you must restore the window first.)

To size a window, first position the pointer on a border. Notice that the corners of the borders are separated from the straight sections by segment boundary lines, as shown in the Paintbrush window in Figure 6-6. If you want to resize the window by moving only one border, position the pointer on that border. To move two borders at once, position the pointer on the corner segment between the two.

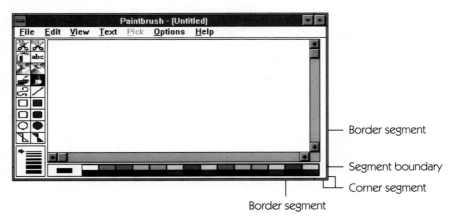

Border segment

Segment boundary

Corner segment

Border segment

FIGURE 6-6. *The window border and corner segments.*

Notice that when the pointer is on a border, it changes to a two-headed arrow. As shown in Figure 6-7, the exact shape of the arrow depends on which border segment the mouse pointer is on. To size the window, press the primary mouse button (usually the left one) and drag the pointer until the window is the desired size. Then release the mouse button.

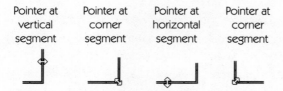

Pointer at vertical segment   Pointer at corner segment   Pointer at horizontal segment   Pointer at corner segment

FIGURE 6-7. *The mouse pointer at different window border segments.*

Try dragging the pointer away from the window's center to enlarge the window. Drag the pointer toward the window's center to shrink the window.

MOVING

Before you can move a window around the screen, the window must be smaller than the size of the screen. If your window is maximized, you must restore it first.

To move a window with the mouse, all you have to do is drag its title bar. You'll notice there's a gray outline to show you where the window is going.

If You Don't Have a Mouse

To maximize, restore, size, and move windows when you don't have a mouse, use the application's Control menu. Press the Alt key and then press the spacebar. This will open the Control menu whether the application is maximized, restored, or minimized.

When the Control menu is open, you can press the X key to maximize an application window that is restored or minimized. You can press the R key to restore an application window that is maximized or minimized. And you can press the N key to minimize an application window that is maximized or restored.

Before an application window can be sized, it must be restored. (You can't size a maximized or minimized window.) Choose the Size command from the Control menu (Alt,spacebar,S). A pointer with four

arrows appears on your computer screen. Press one of the arrow keys on your keyboard to move the pointer to a horizontal or vertical border segment, or press two of the arrow keys (one after the other) to move the pointer to a corner segment. The pointer changes to look like one of the pointers in Figure 6-7. You then press the arrow keys to move the border. When you are done sizing your window, you must press Enter.

Before an application window can be moved, it must be restored. (You can't move a maximized or minimized window.) Choose the Move command from the Control menu (Alt,spacebar,M). A pointer with four arrows appears on your computer screen. Press the arrow keys to position the window where you want it. (As soon as you press an arrow key, the pointer changes to a single arrow.) When you are done moving your window, you must press Enter.

Chapter 7

Working in an Application

Let's get on with it and satisfy your creative urges in Paintbrush. In this chapter you'll use the application's tools and learn how to scroll around in a window. You'll also practice selecting, duplicating, and rearranging parts of a drawing. Then you'll find out how to save, store, and recover your creation.

A drawing program like Paintbrush really does show off the convenience of an operating system like Windows: You can use a mouse to move quickly all over the screen, creating fluid shapes and selecting specific areas of your drawing for change. So the parts of this chapter on drawing and selection will focus on mouse use. If you have a preference for the keyboard, please read the Tip at the end of the chapter titled ''If You Don't Own a Mouse.''

Begin by starting Paintbrush now. If necessary, refer to the section in Chapter 6 called ''Mouse Painting'' for instructions on how to start the application. Figure 7-1 gives you a picture of Paintbrush and identifies parts of the window.

Try drawing a shape. Paintbrush starts out with the Brush tool. Position the mouse pointer (the dot) in the drawing area. Then drag the pointer around the drawing area by holding down the primary (usually the left) mouse button and moving the mouse. To stop drawing, release the mouse button.

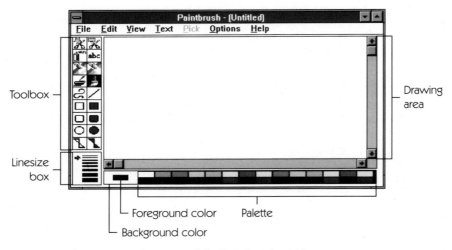

FIGURE 7-1. *The parts of the Paintbrush window.*

SELECTING AND USING A TOOL

As Figure 7-1 shows you, the left side of the Paintbrush window has a toolbox containing two columns of painting tools. When you want to select a tool, you click it. Figure 7-2 identifies four of the Paintbrush tools. Right now try clicking the Rounded Box tool. You'll notice that the box containing the tool's icon changes color. Then move the mouse pointer into the drawing area. Notice that the mouse pointer is now a cross hair (large plus sign). Drag the pointer to draw a box with rounded corners, as shown in Figure 7-3.

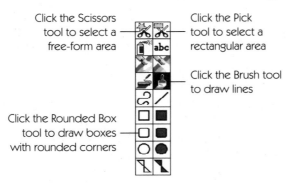

FIGURE 7-2. *Some tools in the Toolbox.*

When the cross hair is here, press the
primary mouse button and drag
toward diagonally opposite corner

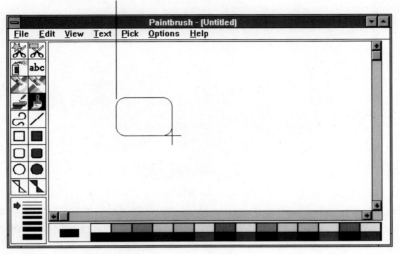

FIGURE 7-3. *Dragging to draw a rounded box.*

MOVING AROUND IN A WINDOW (USING SCROLL BARS)

Anytime a window can't display all the information within the space available, it supplies scroll bars that you can use to move the contents of the window so that the hidden information is revealed. Figure 7-4 shows you how scroll bars are used with a mouse. When you click the lower scroll arrow, you *scroll down*. That is, information below the current, visible contents comes into sight. Notice that the scroll box moves downward as you scroll. When the scroll box is at the bottom of the scroll bar, sitting just above the lower scroll arrow, then you're looking at the end of the information and can scroll no farther. When you click the upper scroll arrow, you *scroll up* so that you see information above the current, visible contents. Now the scroll box moves upward as you scroll. When the scroll box is at the top of the scroll bar, sitting just below the upper scroll arrow, then you're looking at the beginning of the information and can scroll no farther.

Under normal conditions, the Paintbrush window displays scroll bars all the time because the drawing area is larger than the Paintbrush window.

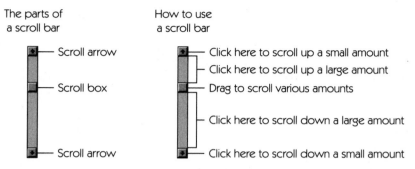

FIGURE 7-4. *The parts of a scroll bar and how to use them.*

SELECTING PART OF YOUR PICTURE

Selecting part of the information in a window is a common action in most applications for Windows. Selecting precedes copying, deleting, moving, or formatting information. When you have selected information, it appears highlighted or enclosed in dotted lines.

To select part of a painting in Paintbrush, first choose either the Pick or Scissors selection tool, shown in Figure 7-2, by clicking it. Again, notice that when you click a tool the box containing the tool's icon changes color.

After you choose a selection tool and move the mouse pointer into the drawing area, the mouse pointer changes to a cross-hair pointer. To select with the Pick tool, drag the pointer to form a rectangle around the area you want to select, as you did to draw a box earlier in the chapter. To select with the Scissors tool, drag the pointer around the shape you want to select. There's an example of each type of selection in Figure 7-5.

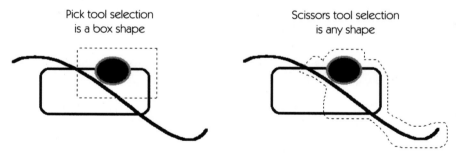

FIGURE 7-5. *The two types of selection in Paintbrush.*

Now that you have selected part (or all) of your painting, you can do a thing or two.

COPYING AND PASTING PICTURE DETAILS

In Windows you can copy selected information from one place and then paste it in another. (Notice that this process uses two different commands—Copy and Paste!) Try out this process in Paintbrush.

1. In the preceding section, you selected part of your painting. That is the first step.

2. Now choose the Copy command from the Edit menu (Alt,E,C or Ctrl+C). Nothing visible happens to your painting. But behind the scenes, Windows makes an electronic copy of your selection and stores the copy in a place called the Clipboard. (The Clipboard is the name for a reserved space in your computer's memory.)

3. To add the copied selection to your painting, choose the Paste command from the Edit menu (Alt,E,P or Ctrl+V). A copy of your selection appears in the upper left corner of the drawing area.

4. Now you can move the pasted copy in the drawing area. Position the pointer in the copy, and then drag the copy where you like.

In Chapter 18, "Common Elements in Applications for Windows," you'll learn more about the Clipboard and how to use it.

SAVING FILES AND OPENING FILES

After you create a painting, you'll probably want to save it in case you want to use it again or change it later. To save your work in any application for Windows, open the File menu and choose the Save command (Alt,F,S). The first time you choose the Save command to save a painting, Paintbrush opens the Save As dialog box, which is shown in Figure 7-6, so that you can give your work a name. You can't save your work in Windows without giving it a name! Your work (with its name) becomes a file in your computer.

NOTE *There are limitations on the kind of name you can give your work. The name can be up to eight characters long, made up of any letters or numbers. You* cannot *use spaces. Some symbols (like the exclamation point, dollar sign, pound sign, percent sign, and underscore) are acceptable; other symbols (like the period, quotation mark, slash, backslash, brackets, colon, semicolon, vertical bar, equal sign, asterisk, and comma) are not acceptable.*

At the end of the name you can add a dot (a period) and an extension of three letters. The extension is often used to identify the application in which a file was created. For example, letters and reports created in the Write application, unless you specify something else, will automatically be given the extension .WRI. You might give a letter to your Uncle Leo the name LEO_LTR.WRI. A name like UNCLE_LEO.WRI would be too long (nine characters in the name), and a name like LEO LTR.WRI would be unacceptable because it contains a space.

In the Save As dialog box, you must also choose a file format. (Different formats are required depending on how the file will be used.) The file format affects the extension; usually your Paintbrush file will have the extension .BMP. (Don't worry about the file formats for now; just use the 16-color format, which is the default on most computers running Windows.)

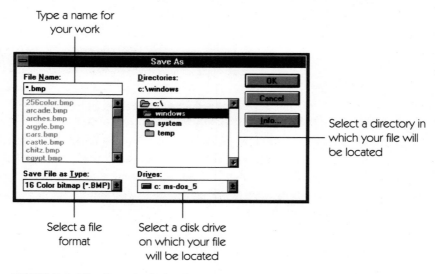

FIGURE 7-6. *The Save As dialog box.*

In the Save As dialog box you also choose a place in your computer (disk drive and directory) where your file will be saved. Look for the file in this location when you need it later.

To save your work—say, it's a picture of a white dog—type a name like DOG1 and then choose OK. Without further instruction, Paintbrush assumes this is a *16-color bitmap* file and names the file DOG1.BMP. If you make more changes to the painting and want to save the changes, choose the Save command again. This time Paintbrush doesn't display a dialog box because you already supplied a name for the work. If you have added spots to the dog and chosen Save, you have a spotted dog in DOG1.BMP. The picture of the white dog no longer exists.

NOTE *You'll learn more about how to use different parts of the dialog box later in this chapter. If you try experimenting now and get confused, click the Cancel button in the dialog box or press the Esc key. The dialog box will close without making any changes to what was previously in your computer.*

You also have the option of saving the changed painting with a different name. To do so, choose the Save As command from the File menu (Alt,F,A), which displays the same Save As dialog box you saw when you first chose Save. You then type a new name for the changed work and choose OK to save the changes with a different name.

Here's an example of what happens when you save your changes with a different name. Your file DOG1.BMP has a picture of a spotted dog. This has been saved. If you erase the spots and make your dog black, you can choose the Save As command and name this file DOG2.BMP. You now have two files in your computer: DOG1.BMP has a picture of a spotted dog, and DOG2.BMP has a picture of a black dog.

After you've saved your work, it resides in a file on a disk. With your work saved, you can safely quit Paintbrush and Windows and turn off your computer. The next time you start your computer and Windows, you can start Paintbrush again and then retrieve the work so that you can work on it some more. To retrieve work that is in the computer but not visible in an application window, open the file that contains the work. The application then displays your work in a window.

To work on a painting that is saved but not visible in a window, open the File menu and choose the Open command (Alt,F,O).

The Open dialog box is shown in Figure 7-7. In it you identify the location of your file (drive and directory) and identify the file type. Then you can type the name of the file or choose the file from the list by clicking its name. You choose OK to display your work in the Paintbrush window.

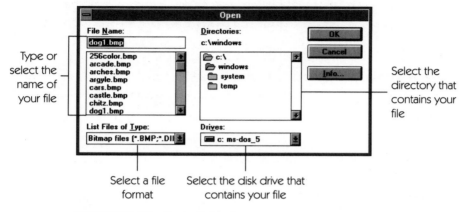

FIGURE 7-7. *The Open dialog box.*

You now have some insight into the flow of work in an application: After creating a drawing (or letter or spreadsheet), you save it using the Save As dialog box, and you retrieve it later using the Open dialog box. The rest of this chapter gives you some general information about the workings of these and other dialog boxes.

MORE ABOUT DIALOG BOXES

A dialog box has text boxes and other elements in it. When you open a dialog box, one of these elements will be highlighted or surrounded by a dotted box. When you open the Save As dialog box, for example, the text box for naming your file is highlighted. You can type a name right away.

As you learned in Chapter 5 in the section called ''Making Changes in Dialog Boxes,'' there are several ways of accessing the different elements in a dialog box. With the mouse, you click the element you want to change. With the keyboard, you press Tab to cycle through the elements. You can also use the keyboard to jump directly to an element by holding down the Alt key and, while holding down the Alt key, pressing the letter key that matches the underlined letter in the element's name.

This chapter describes the elements that you'll find in a Save As or Open dialog box. You'll learn about other types of dialog box elements as they come up in the course of this book.

Dialog Box Elements

The elements in the Save As dialog box are labeled in Figure 7-8.

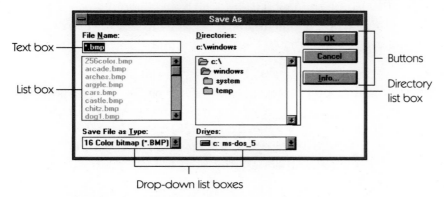

FIGURE 7-8. *The elements in the Save As dialog box.*

Text box

In a text box, you type words or numbers. In the Save As dialog box, for example, you type a filename for the work you want to save. In the Open dialog box (see Figure 7-7), you type the filename of the work you want to open and work on.

List box

A list box displays a list of choices. For example, the list box in Figure 7-8 gives a list of existing filenames. You select from a list box by clicking the choice or by pressing the up or down arrow key to move the highlight to the choice. If you double-click a choice in a list box, two things happen: First, that choice is selected, and second, Windows performs the task associated with the dialog box's default button. (See the "Buttons" section below for a description of the default button.)

Notice that in the Save As dialog box, all the names in the list box are grayed, which lets you know that you should be careful about using those names because they have already been used.

Directory list box

A directory list box displays a list of icons representing different locations (called directories) in your computer. You use these locations to organize and find your files. Chapter 10, "Managing Files," explains in detail what directories are and how you use them. The directory list box enables you to access any directory in your computer. It's important that you know how to use the directory list box, but to use it you must understand the concepts discussed in Chapter 10. You'll find a description of how to use the directory list box in Chapter 18 in the section "Opening an Existing Work File."

Scroll bars

In a list box that contains more choices than can appear on the screen at one time, Windows adds a scroll bar. The scroll bar in a list box works in exactly the same way as a scroll bar in a window. Click a scroll arrow, click between a scroll arrow and the scroll box, or drag the scroll box to see other parts of the list. You can also press the up and down arrow keys to move the highlight through the list.

Drop-down list boxes

At the bottom of the Save As and Open dialog boxes, there are two drop-down list boxes. In the Open dialog box, one is labeled List Files as Type and the other is labeled Drives. You use these two boxes to change the list of choices in the File Name list box. To use a drop-down list box, click the down arrow button at the right end of the box. This action opens a list. You can then make a selection. Or, with the keyboard, press Tab to move the highlight to the drop-down list, press the down arrow key to drop the list down, and then press the up or down arrow key to highlight your choice. Whether you use the mouse or the keyboard to select, your choice will be shown in the text box portion of the element.

To close a drop-down list box, click the down arrow button again with your mouse, or press the Alt+up arrow or the Alt+down arrow key.

Buttons

Buttons cause an action to be performed. Most dialog boxes have at least two standard buttons—OK and Cancel. The Save As and Open dialog boxes in Paintbrush contain an additional button labeled Info. When you choose the Info button, Paintbrush displays a box that lists some statistics about the selected painting, as shown in Figure 7-9.

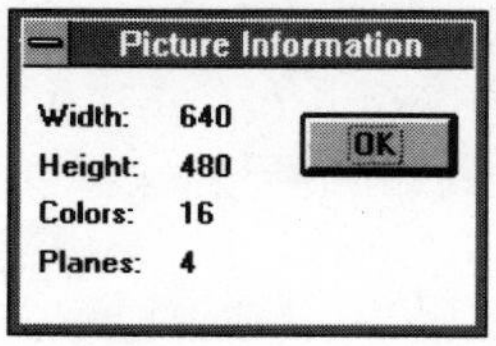

FIGURE 7-9. *A sample Info box.*

From the Save As dialog box, the Info box displays statistics about the painting you are saving. From the Open dialog box, the Info box displays statistics about the painting you have selected in the File Name list box. In the Info box, you can't type or select any options. The box only displays information. You can only choose OK to close the Info box.

If you look carefully at the buttons shown in Figure 7-8, you'll see that the OK button has a black border that is thicker than the borders of the other two buttons. This border indicates that the OK button is the default button. When you press the Enter key, Windows performs the action associated with the default button. The default button is most often the OK button, but it can vary.

Closing a Dialog Box

To close a dialog box, you'll usually choose either the OK button or the Cancel button. The OK button closes the dialog box and directs the application to perform the action specified in the dialog box. The Cancel button (or pressing the Esc key) closes the dialog box and initiates no action.

In some dialog boxes, you will see buttons that perform actions and leave the dialog box open so that you can do more. In these cases, the Cancel button usually changes to a Close button. Choosing the Close button (or pressing the Esc key) closes the dialog box and leaves in place the actions taken so far.

MESSAGE BOXES

From time to time, Windows and applications need to provide you with information. Sometimes you need to know that an action could not be performed. Sometimes you need to know that an action was completed successfully. To provide information, Windows displays message boxes.

In most ways, a message box acts like a dialog box that contains only buttons. Paintbrush displays the message box shown in Figure 7-10 if you try to exit the application without saving your work. If you choose the Yes button, Paintbrush saves your work and then quits. If you choose the No button, Paintbrush simply quits, and your changes are lost. And if you choose the Cancel button, you cancel the command to quit and return to Paintbrush. By using a message box, Paintbrush helps you avoid the mistake of not saving your work of art.

FIGURE 7-10. *A typical Windows message box.*

If You Don't Own a Mouse

To use Paintbrush with a keyboard, you must press the Tab key to move between the Toolbox, Linesize box, Palette, and drawing area. Within each of these four areas, the arrow keys are your way of moving the cursor around. The Ins (short for "Insert") key is your substitute for the left mouse button when you want to "click" to make a selection or "drag" to draw or erase.

You learned in Chapter 5, in the section "Using the Keyboard," how to use the keyboard in text boxes. The section "More About Dialog Boxes" in this chapter discusses how to use the keyboard with additional dialog box elements.

Chapter 8

Arranging Icons and Windows

You already know how to find your way in Program Manager and between your applications. But sometimes your screen can get disorganized, making it hard to remember which icons are available and which applications are running. With many applications running at once in the Windows operating system, it's easy to have a screen full of icons and windows. Chapter 3, "Starting Out, Finding Your Way, and Quitting," suggests you minimize group windows and quit applications, if necessary, to help you find your way around. This chapter discusses alternative ways of staying organized, by arranging the icons and windows on your screen.

ARRANGING ICONS AND WINDOWS IN PROGRAM MANAGER

Within Program Manager, you can arrange the icons in an open group window by first switching to that window (so that it's the active window) and then opening the Window menu and choosing the Arrange Icons command (Alt,W,A). In addition to arranging the icons in neat rows and columns within a group window, this command provides an additional convenience. Before you choose the Arrange Icons command, a group window might contain both horizontal and vertical scroll bars. To see all the icons in this case, you have to scroll in two directions, as shown in Figure 8-1.

FIGURE 8-1. *The Accessories group window with two scroll bars.*

After you choose the Arrange Icons command (Alt,W,A), Windows arranges the icons into the number of columns that fit within the width of the group window. This arrangement eliminates the need for a horizontal scroll bar. To see all the icons after rearrangement, you need only scroll vertically. See Figure 8-2.

FIGURE 8-2. *The Accessories group window after rearrangement, with only a vertical scroll bar.*

Within Program Manager, you can also arrange the group windows by choosing one of several commands on the Window menu. If you choose the Cascade command (Alt,W,C), the open group windows will be sized and arranged so that the windows overlap, leaving each group window's title bar visible. (But if there isn't room in the Program Manager for all the group windows to cascade, they will cascade into a second row on top of the first.) See Figure 8-3. The minimized group windows are aligned at the bottom of the Program Manager window.

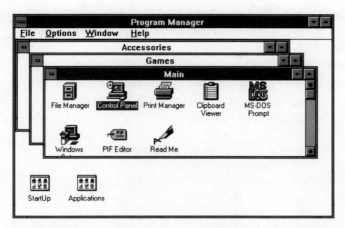

FIGURE 8-3. *The arrangement of group windows after you choose the Cascade command.*

If you choose the Tile command from the Window menu (Alt,W,T), the open group windows will be sized and arranged side by side so that as much as possible of each window is visible in the Program Manager window. See Figure 8-4. The minimized group windows are aligned at the bottom of the Program Manager window.

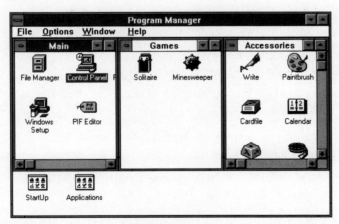

FIGURE 8-4. *The arrangement of group windows after you choose the Tile command.*

ARRANGING APPLICATION ICONS AND WINDOWS WITH THE TASK LIST

In addition to arranging icons and group windows in Program Manager, you will also undoubtedly want to arrange the application icons and windows on your screen. You can easily organize your screen by using the Task List. As you can see in Figure 8-5, the Task List is a dialog box that can be used to perform many different operations.

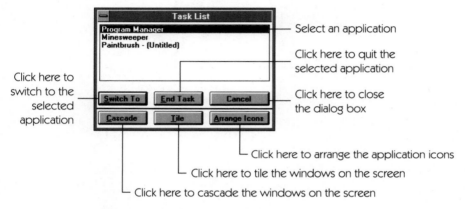

FIGURE 8-5. *The Task List dialog box.*

But how do you get to the Task List? Windows makes it easy to use the Task List by providing three ways to access it:

- With the mouse, you can double-click in any blank space visible on the screen to display the Task List. (A blank space is an area not covered by a window or an icon.)

- With the keyboard, you can press the Ctrl+Esc key combination. You don't need to have blank space available on the screen.

- Or you can choose the Switch To command from any application's Control menu (Alt,spacebar,W).

When you have the Task List open, you can use it to arrange the application icons (icons of minimized applications). The Arrange Icons button will place application icons in a neat row at the bottom of the screen. You can also arrange application icons manually by dragging them with the mouse.

In addition, you can use the Task List to arrange the application windows on the screen. If you choose the Cascade button, the windows will be sized and arranged so that the windows overlap, leaving each window's title bar visible. (But if there isn't room for all the applications to cascade in one row, they will start cascading in a second row on top of the first.) If you choose the Tile button, the windows on the screen will be sized and arranged side by side so that each window is visible. Figure 8-6 shows four windows after the Cascade button was chosen. Figure 8-7 shows the same windows after the Tile button was chosen. Notice that Windows leaves room at the bottom of the screen for the application icons.

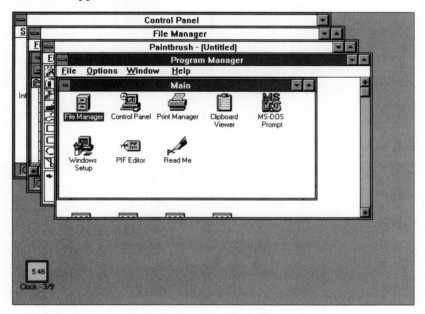

FIGURE 8-6. *The arrangement of four windows after you choose the Cascade button in the Task List.*

The Task List is also useful for switching between applications, as an alternative to using the mouse or the Alt+Tab key combination. The list box in the Task List dialog box displays the names of all the applications that are currently running. (If you have more than seven applications running, the list box will contain a scroll bar.) To switch to an application, select its name in

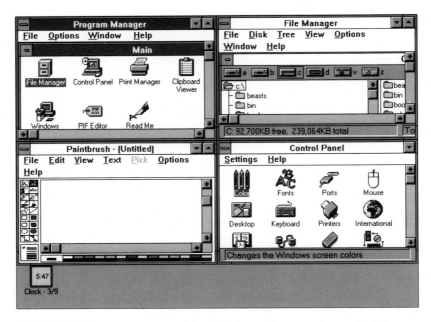

FIGURE 8-7. *The arrangement of four windows after you choose the Tile button in the Task List.*

the list box and then choose the Switch To button from the Task List dialog box. The Task List then disappears and the application you selected comes to the front.

If you choose the End Task button after selecting an application in the Task List, Windows quits the application. If you choose the Cancel button in the Task List, the Task List dialog box disappears, and you return to the application you were using when you opened the Task List.

Chapter 9

Getting Help

As you work in the Windows operating system, you can find out what you want to know about Windows and about individual applications without having to leave your computer to rummage through reference books. You press a key: F1. The F1 key displays Help information about the application you are using. Help is a separate application with its own window. See Figure 9-1.

FIGURE 9-1. *The Help window with a list of topics about Program Manager.*

One advantage of using the F1 key to access Help is that the information you get is specific to the current task. For example, pressing the F1 key while a dialog box is visible usually yields information about the dialog box and the command that displayed it, as shown in Figure 9-2.

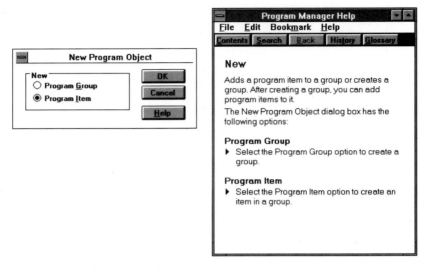

FIGURE 9-2. *A screen of Help information about a dialog box.*

Another way to get help is by choosing a command from the Help menu. You'll find the Help menu on an application's menu bar. See Figure 9-3 for an example. The Help menu's Contents command brings up Help with a list of different Help topics from which you can choose. For this reason, the Help menu is especially handy when you want to browse.

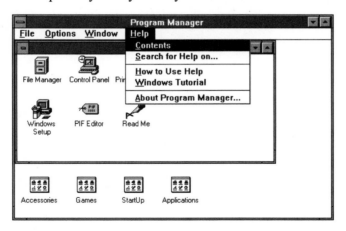

FIGURE 9-3. *The Help menu in Program Manager.*

Whether you press the F1 key or choose a topic through the Help menu, Windows displays the information in the same window, in the same way. Once in Help, however you get there, you can use buttons and commands to get to the Contents screen, to jump to related topics, to browse, or to find the definition of a term, name, or label. The following sections explain these features of Help.

JUMPING TO TOPICS IN HELP

In many Help windows, you see underlined words, as shown in Figure 9-1. On color screens, the underlined words usually appear in green letters too. These underlined words often describe related topics. To make a jump to Help information about one of these topics, use the mouse to click the underlined words. Notice that the mouse pointer changes to a hand shape when you position it over underlined words.

To make a jump with the keyboard, press the Tab key until the underlined words you want to select are highlighted. When the underlined words are highlighted, press Enter. Figure 9-4 shows the Help window before a jump to the topic *Change an Icon*. Figure 9-5 shows the Help window after the jump.

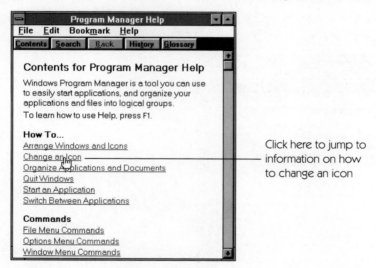

FIGURE 9-4. *Preparing to jump to a topic.*

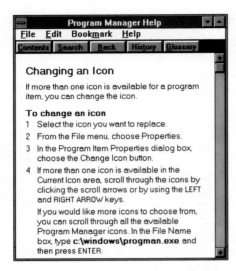

FIGURE 9-5. *The topic indicated in Figure 9-4.*

You will also occasionally see words and phrases with dotted underlines in the Help window. When you click one of these, Help gives a definition of the word or phrase in a small box. Figure 9-6 shows the definition that appears when you click the words *title bar*. To close the box containing the definition, click anywhere on the screen or press any key.

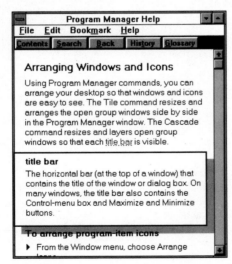

FIGURE 9-6. *The definition that appears when you click the underlined phrase* title bar.

USING THE BUTTONS IN HELP

You've probably noticed that the Help window has a row of buttons below the menu bar. See Figure 9-7.

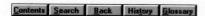

FIGURE 9-7. *The buttons in Program Manager's Help window.*

The Contents, Search, Back, History, and Glossary buttons enable you to "travel" from screen to screen of Help until you find the exact information you need. Figure 9-8 summarizes what each button does.

Button	What It Does
Contents	Displays the list of Help topics for a particular application. You can jump from a topic to specific information.
Search	Gives you a way to search for specific information. When you start typing in the Search text box, Help displays in the list box the available topics that are similarly spelled.
Back	Shows you the topic you were looking at before you jumped to the topic you are looking at now. You can continue retracing your steps through Help.
History	Displays a list of all the topics you have looked at since you started Help (up to 40 topics). You can jump from any topic in the list to its Help screen.
Glossary	Displays a list of defined terms. You can view a definition by clicking the term. You can keep the Glossary window running and minimized at the bottom of your screen as long as Help is running.

FIGURE 9-8. *The Help buttons and what they do.*

USING THE ABOUT COMMAND

On the Help menu shown in Figure 9-3, notice the command called About Program Manager. This command displays a message box that gives you some useful information, as shown in Figure 9-9. The numbers at the bottom of the message box vary depending on the type of computer you are using and on the number of applications you are running.

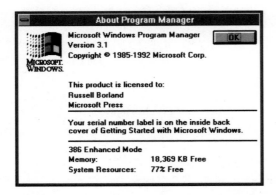

FIGURE 9-9. *The About Program Manager message box.*

All applications for Windows provide an About command. Some of the applications, like Program Manager, provide information on available memory and disk space. Some programs display only the version number of the application and copyright information. But remember: If you need to check on memory or disk space, you can always switch to Program Manager and use the About Program Manager command.

QUITTING HELP

You quit Help in the same way you quit any application. Double-click the Control-menu box (or, with the keyboard, use the Alt+F4 key combination).

Chapter 10

Managing Files

So far in this book you've encountered one kind of hierarchy, one that has Program Manager at the top, with a variety of applications at the next level (applications that are organized within Program Manager), followed by any number of work files at the third level (files that are created within each application).

Right now, to understand the organization inside your computer, you have to look at the components of the Windows operating system in a totally new way. Program Manager and other applications are program files, and they are stored inside your computer along with the files you create. From this perspective, Program Manager, other applications, and work files are pretty much equivalent and are not at different levels of a hierarchy. They are all files that are contained in your computer.

There is a new hierarchy that you have to understand: a view of the space inside your computer where information (such as program files and work files) is contained. For the storage of program files, work files, and other information, you'll find that the space inside your computer is divided into sections, and maybe subsections, and maybe sub-subsections, and so on, like the trunk, branches, smaller branches, and leaves of a tree. See the illustration in Figure 10-1. The biggest branches in your computer are the disk drives, the next smaller size branches are directories, and then there are subdirectories. The leaves of the tree are the programs, work files, and other files. Within this structure of directories and subdirectories are the locations to which you save your work files and from which you retrieve them. Each file is contained in a directory or subdirectory. Your computer is divided this way to make it possible to organize its contents. For example, you could save all your letters in a subdirectory called *LETTERS*. Then when you want to retrieve a letter, you'll know exactly where to find it.

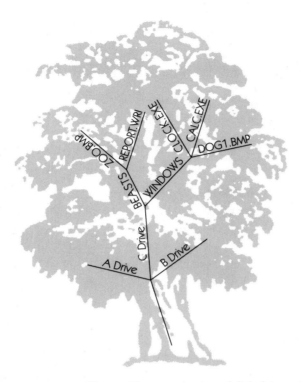

FIGURE 10-1. *The treelike organization of disk drives, directories, and files.*

This view of the organization inside your computer is important because sometimes you need to look through this *directory tree* to find a file, or you might want to move or copy a file from one directory location to another so you can find it later. These and other tasks are accomplished easily from within File Manager and are discussed in this chapter. (Chapter 14, ''More About File Manager,'' describes additional features.)

SWINGING THROUGH THE DIRECTORY TREES

Start File Manager now. You'll find its icon in the Main group window in Program Manager. Figure 10-2 shows you the File Manager window. The disk drive inside your computer, where most of your program files and work files are stored, is commonly designated as the C drive. In Figure 10-2, the C drive is the drive being displayed in a window. You can look at the directories in a different drive by clicking that drive's icon at the top of the window.

Disk drive icons

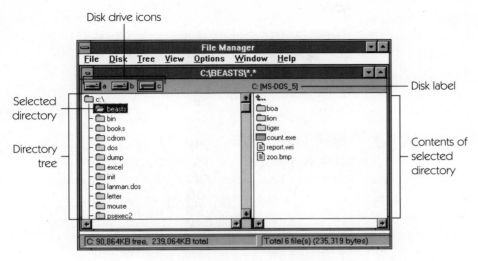

FIGURE 10-2. *The File Manager window showing the C drive with an open folder.*

You'll notice that the window in File Manager is divided into two parts, called *panes*. The directories and various files are all represented by different icons. (These icons are explained in Figure 10-3.) The pane on the left is the *directory-tree* pane, and it shows the levels of directories on a disk. In Figure 10-2 you can see that one of those directories is selected, as represented by an open-folder icon. The pane on the right, called the *directory-contents* pane, shows the contents of the selected directory. To open a directory and view its contents, you can either click the folder in the directory-tree pane or double-click the folder in the directory-contents pane.

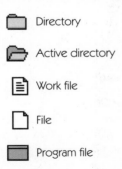

Directory

Active directory

Work file

File

Program file

FIGURE 10-3. *The File Manager icons.*

To move around the directory tree, you click the directory whose contents you want to view. If you prefer to use the keyboard to move around the directory tree, see the Tip called "If You Don't Have a Mouse," at the end of this chapter.

EXPANDING AND COLLAPSING YOUR VIEW OF THE BRANCHES

When you first start File Manager, the directory tree in the left pane shows what's known as the root directory of the disk drive (for example, C:\) and the first level of directories attached to the root directory. You can expand or collapse your view of the directory tree to show more or fewer directories at various levels. To increase your understanding of how the directory tree works, go to the Tree menu and choose the Indicate Expandable Branches command (Alt,T,I). (Don't choose this command if it already has a check mark next to it.) You'll notice that some directory icons now have a plus sign on them, some have a minus sign, and some are blank, as shown in Figure 10-4. A plus sign means that a directory has subdirectories in it that aren't shown. If you double-click the folder, the tree will expand, as shown in Figure 10-5. A minus sign means that the view is already expanded; double-clicking that folder will cause the view of the tree to contract to its original level of detail. If a directory icon has neither a plus sign nor a minus sign, that directory has no subdirectories.

Double-click to expand the view —

FIGURE 10-4. *A collapsed view of a directory.*

Double-click
to collapse
the view

FIGURE 10-5. *An expanded view of a directory.*

Double-clicking folders expands and collapses your view of the directory tree whether or not you have chosen the Indicate Expandable Branches command. If you want to see the entire tree expanded, you can choose the Expand All command from the Tree menu (Alt,T,A).

VIEWING TWO DIRECTORY TREES (USING NEW WINDOW AND TILE COMMANDS)

To simultaneously look at the contents of two different directories on the same disk drive, you first have to open a new window in File Manager. You'll find that the multiple windows in File Manager work a lot like the group windows in Program Manager. You can arrange the windows inside File Manager or switch between them in the same ways you arrange and switch between the group windows in Program Manager. The main difference is that any window inside File Manager can be closed, as long as one window inside File Manager remains open. You minimize windows in File Manager with the Minimize button or the Minimize command on the Control menu. You close windows in File Manager by double-clicking in the Control-menu box or by pressing Ctrl+F4.

To open a new window in File Manager, choose the New Window command from the Window menu (Alt,W,N). Try it. The new window is there, but you won't be able to see all the contents of both windows because the new window is on top of the old one. Next choose the Tile command from the Window menu (Alt,W,T). File Manager tiles the two windows, which means it sizes and arranges them to share (and fill) the available space. See Figure 10-6 for an example.

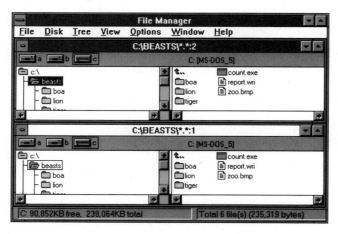

FIGURE 10-6. *Two tiled windows within File Manager showing views of the same directory tree and contents.*

You can open more windows if you want. Try choosing the New Window command again (Alt,W,N); a new window opens on top of the others. Choose the Tile command again (Alt,W,T), and you see the three windows arranged to share the available space.

To return to just one view of your directory tree, you'll have to close two of the windows. Double-click the Control-menu box of each of the windows you want to close; or move to a window using Ctrl+Tab and press Ctrl+F4.

In any open window within File Manager, you can view the contents of any disk drive in your computer. When you click a drive icon near the top of the File Manager window, File Manager replaces the window contents with a view of the drive you specified.

Suppose, however, that you're looking at the directory tree of your C disk drive and want to compare it to the directory tree of your A drive, but you only have one window open within File Manager. You can double-click the A-drive icon and then choose Tile (Alt,W,T). Now you should have a view of each drive, as shown in Figure 10-7.

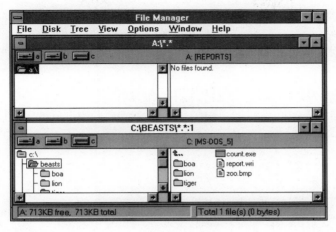

FIGURE 10-7. *Two windows within File Manager showing views of the directory trees on different disk drives.*

Changing the File Manager Window

You can change the display of information in the File Manager window. With the mouse, you place the mouse pointer between the two panes of the window so that the pointer changes shape, as shown in the first picture below. When you drag the mouse, the split bar (a black vertical line) appears. By dragging the split bar you can change the relative size of the panes or close one pane completely, as shown on the following page.

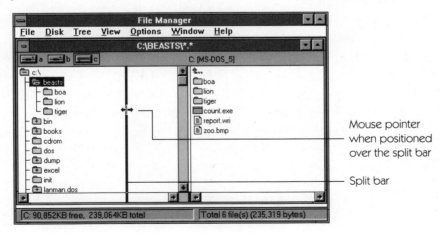

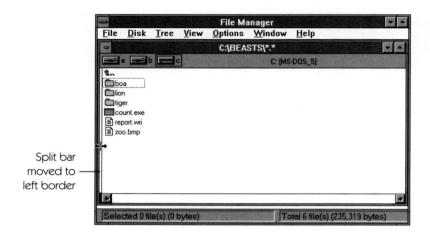

Split bar
moved to
left border

With the keyboard, you can choose commands from the View menu to close one of the two panes or change their relative sizes. You can choose the Tree Only command (Alt,V,E) to close the directory-contents pane, or the Directory Only command (Alt,V,O) to close the directory-tree pane, or the Split command (Alt,V,L) to change the relative sizes of the two panes.

COPYING AND MOVING FILES AND DIRECTORIES

Two important tasks you perform with File Manager are copying and moving files and directories. (In the case of a directory, files and subdirectories contained in the directory are also copied or moved.) When you copy a file or directory, File Manager leaves the original where it was and puts a copy of it where you specify. When you move a file or directory, the original is moved to the location you specify, and no copy is left behind. File Manager makes these two tasks very easy, especially if you have a mouse. You can copy and move files and directories to locations in the same disk drive or to locations in a different disk drive. The table in Figure 10-8 summarizes the mouse techniques for copying and moving files and directories, as explained in the sections that follow. (For keyboard information, see the Tip called ''If You Don't Have a Mouse,'' at the end of this chapter.)

Mouse Action	Destination	Effect on Files and Directories
Ctrl+drag	The same disk drive	Copies the files and directories
Drag	The same disk drive	Moves the files and directories
Drag	A different disk drive	Copies the files and directories
Shift+drag	A different disk drive	Moves the files and directories

FIGURE 10-8. *Summary of mouse actions for copying and moving files and directories.*

Copying and Moving a File or Directory on the Same Drive

To *copy* a file or directory to a new location on the same drive, press the Ctrl key and, while holding down the Ctrl key, drag the file or directory icon to the directory icon where you want the copy. You'll see an image of a file icon (with a plus sign in it) move with the mouse pointer as you drag. As you drag the pointer over a potential destination directory, you'll see a box around both the directory icon and its name. Release the mouse button when there's a box around the directory you want to copy the file or folder to. See Figure 10-9. If you drag the file or directory to the directory in which it currently resides, File Manager informs you that it can't copy files when the destination is the same as the source.

To *move* a file or directory, drag the file or directory folder icon to the directory folder icon where you want to move the file. Unlike copying, do not use the Ctrl key when you want to move a file or directory. Notice that when you move a file or directory, the icon next to its name disappears when you begin to drag it. Also, the icon contains no plus sign. These indicators let you know that you are moving and not copying. If you drag the file or directory to the directory in which it currently resides, File Manager informs you that it can't move files when the destination is the same as the source.

87

File to be copied

Source
directory of
the file

Destination
directory of
the file

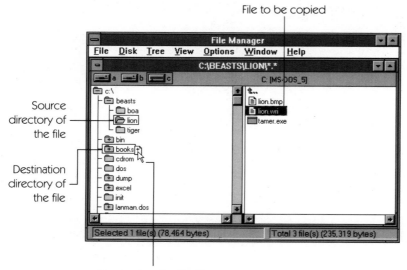

Mouse dragging the file

FIGURE 10-9. *Dragging a file from its source directory to create a copy in a new directory.*

TIP

Copying Files to the Clipboard

The Copy dialog box (displayed when you choose Copy from the File menu) contains an option button for copying a file to the Clipboard. This dialog box is shown on the next page. To select the option button, click the circle where it says "Copy to Clipboard." A dot will appear in the circle. This option lets you place the contents of an entire file on the Clipboard without having to go through the process of starting an application, opening the file, selecting the entire contents, and then copying the selection to the Clipboard. This option can be very handy if you are working in a document into which you want to insert the entire contents of another file. And it's especially handy in applications that let you open only one window at a time.

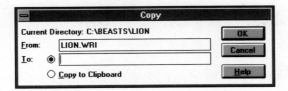

Copying and Moving a File or Directory to a Different Drive

To *copy* a file or directory to a different drive, drag the file or directory icon to the disk-drive icon where you want the copy. The icon you drag has a plus sign in it. If the destination drive has more than one directory, you need to open a window for that disk drive first so that you can drag the file or directory icon to the directory where you want the copy. Refer to the earlier section, "Viewing Two Directory Trees," for directions on how to display two windows at once.

To *move* a file or directory, use the same procedure except that you have to hold down the Shift key while you're dragging the file or directory folder icon to its destination. The icon you drag will contain no plus sign.

FORMATTING AND LABELING FLOPPY DISKS

Floppy disks (sometimes called external disks) require special processing to prepare them for use. Before you can use one, you must format the disk so that it can store files and directories. File Manager provides a command for formatting disks. After you format a disk, you can also give the disk a label. The label is a handy way to show you the kind of information stored on the disk.

Formatting a Floppy Disk

To format a floppy disk, insert the disk in a floppy-disk drive. Then click the drive icon for drive C. You cannot format a disk if the disk drive's contents are being displayed in an active File Manager window. You can format disks in any other disk drive. By clicking the drive icon for drive C, you assure that you can format a floppy disk in any floppy-disk drive.

After you insert a disk in a floppy-disk drive and click the C-drive icon, choose the Format Disk command from the Disk menu (Alt,D,F). The Format Disk command displays the dialog box shown in Figure 10-10.

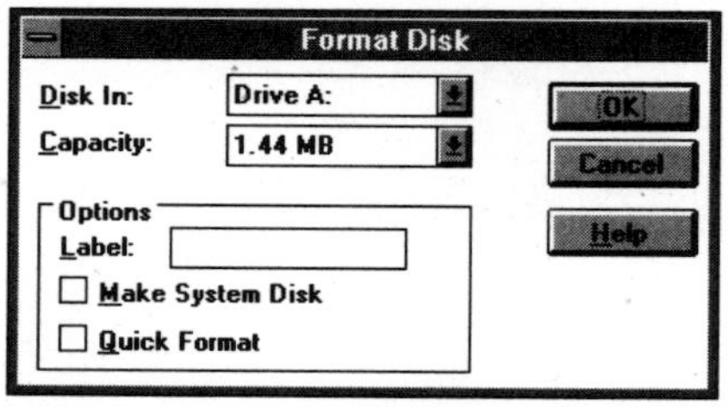

FIGURE 10-10. *The Format Disk dialog box.*

File Manager automatically selects the highest capacity that the disk drive can handle. If you need to format the disk at a lower capacity, click the Capacity drop-down list box and select the density you need. For example, if you have a high-density disk drive (1.2 MB) and you want to make a disk for a colleague who has a low-density disk drive (360 KB), you would select 360K.

You can type a label for the disk now or add a label later (see the next section). A label is a one-word electronic name for the disk. The label can match or be different from the paper label you affix to the outside of the disk.

The Make System Disk check box directs File Manager to add files that can be used to start a computer. You'll almost never need to use this check box.

The Quick Format check box works only for disks that you have formatted already and want to format again. If you try to format a new (never before formatted) disk with the Quick Format check box turned on, File Manager will display a message box after you begin the process that asks if you want to proceed with normal formatting.

When the options in the dialog box suit your needs, choose the OK button. File Manager immediately displays a message box warning you that all data will be erased from the disk you're formatting and giving you a chance to cancel the process. If you're certain that you want the disk formatted, choose the Yes button in the message box. If not, choose No.

Labeling Later

If you decided not to give a disk an electronic label when you formatted it, you can add a label later. Also, you can change the label on any disk, even a hard disk, at any time. (This ability to change a disk's electronic label is very handy when you inherit a computer that has its hard disk labeled already or that has no label.)

To add an electronic label to a disk, go to a window in File Manager that displays the contents of the disk drive. Then choose the Label Disk command from the Disk menu (Alt,D,L).

After you choose the command, File Manager displays the dialog box shown in Figure 10-11. Check the name in the Label text box to be sure you are changing the label of the correct disk. You don't want to change the label of the wrong disk, do you? Type a new name or edit the current name. Choose the OK button to change the label. You will see the new label in the upper right corner of the File Manager window.

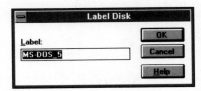

FIGURE 10-11. *The Label Disk dialog box.*

If You Don't Have a Mouse

To move from one part of File Manager to another with the keyboard, press the Tab key. The Tab key will move you from the directory-tree pane to the directory-contents pane to the disk-drive icons.

In the directory-tree pane, you can open a directory (so that its contents are displayed in the directory-contents pane) by pressing the letter key that matches the first letter of the directory name. If a disk contains more than one directory with the same initial letter, another press of the matching letter key will open the next directory beginning with that letter. You can also press the up and down arrow keys to open directories. The name of the currently open directory will be highlighted. To expand your view of a collapsed directory or to collapse your view of an expanded directory, move the highlight to the directory and press Enter.

To view the contents of a different disk drive, press the Ctrl key and then press the letter of the drive you'd like to see. If you'd like to open a new window containing the contents of a different disk drive, press Tab until one of the drive icons is highlighted. Then use the arrow keys to select the disk drive you want and press Enter.

It's not hard to move or copy files and directories using the keyboard, but you have to use MS-DOS directory notation to specify the file destination (e.g., C:\WINDOWS\DOG1.BMP). First select the file or directory that you would like to move or copy. Then go to the File menu in File Manager and choose either the Move command (Alt,F,M or F7) or the Copy command (Alt,F,C or F8). Type the name of the destination directory in the text box labeled To *and press Enter.*

Chapter 11

Creating Your Own Work Space

One of the great joys of using the Windows operating system is setting up Windows to suit yourself. You can make Windows as individual and as well organized as your desk and work space.

In this chapter you will learn how to set up a clock, a calendar, and a card file, and how to decorate Windows to please you. Figure 11-1 shows one Windows arrangement.

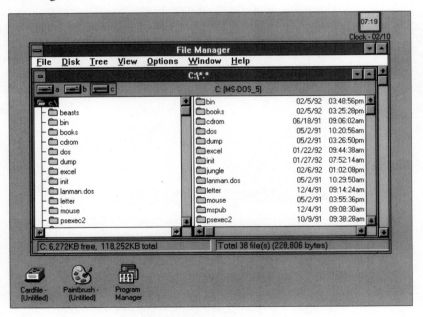

FIGURE 11-1. *A workaday Windows arrangement.*

SETTING UP A CLOCK

Without being a "clock watcher," you probably use a clock throughout the day, so that you know when to go to meetings, deliver reports, catch the last mail pickup, or leave work to pick up your child. Windows provides Clock (Figure 11-2), an application that displays the time of day and the date.

Go ahead and start Clock. Its icon can be found in the Accessories group window. (You learned how to start applications from Program Manager in Chapter 3, "Starting Out, Finding Your Way, and Quitting.")

FIGURE 11-2. *Now you have the time.*

Setting Clock's Date and Time

Clock displays the date and time of your computer's internal clock. If the date or time isn't correct in your computer, Clock will display incorrect information. To set the date and time, start Control Panel from Program Manager's Main group window. Figure 11-3 shows you the Control Panel window. Double-click the Date/Time icon.

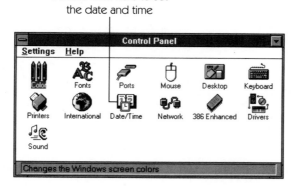

FIGURE 11-3. *The Control Panel window contains the Date/Time icon.*

After you double-click the Date/Time icon in Control Panel, you can set the date and time in the Date & Time dialog box, as shown in Figure 11-4. Double-click any number, and either type a new number or click the arrows (the up-pointing and down-pointing triangles located to the right of the date and time) to make the number larger or smaller. (To review methods for changing numbers in a text box, refer to the section ''Making Changes in Dialog Boxes'' in Chapter 5.) You can also move to different numbers in the Date & Time dialog box with the Tab key.

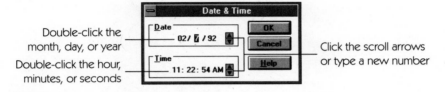

FIGURE 11-4. *The Date & Time dialog box.*

After you set the correct date and time and choose OK, quit Control Panel by double-clicking the Control-menu box on the title bar. Clock now shows the correct date and time.

Other Clock Settings

Let's look again at Clock. The one menu on Clock's menu bar is called *Settings*. The menu is open in Figure 11-5. With the commands on this menu you can customize your clock. For example, you can choose between a clock with hands and a clock with just numbers. To switch the clock face from numbers to hands, choose the Analog command (Alt,S,A). To switch the clock face from hands to numbers, choose the Digital command (Alt,S,D).

FIGURE 11-5. *The Settings menu in Clock.*

One valuable piece of information: If you choose the No Title command, Clock's title bar will disappear. You may wonder how to get it back. Double-click the clock face to make the title bar reappear.

Keeping Your Clock on Top

When you're working in an application with its window maximized, the window takes up the entire screen, making it impossible to see Clock. Wouldn't it be nice to put Clock or its icon (which also shows you the time) in a corner of the screen so that you can see it any time, even while you're working in a maximized window? Clock gives you this option, as shown in Figure 11-6. To make Clock visible at all times, choose the Always On Top command from Clock's Control menu (Alt,spacebar,T).

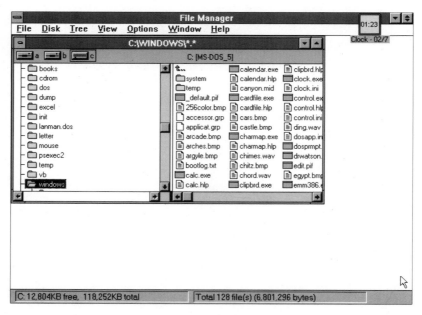

FIGURE 11-6. *A maximized window with the Clock icon on top.*

DECORATING THE WALLS AND WINDOWS

You'll be surprised how colorfully Windows can be decorated! You can display *wallpaper* and a *desktop pattern* in the background. You can change the colors of many parts of a window and the screen. You can also have Windows display animated patterns (called *screen savers*) on your computer screen when you are away from your work for a while. To do your decorating you'll have to start Control Panel from the Main group window in Program Manager. Then you'll need to double-click the Desktop icon. See Figure 11-7.

Double-click here to set wallpaper,
desktop pattern, and screen saver

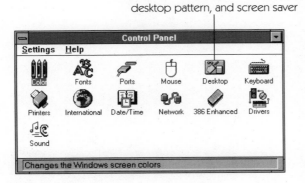

FIGURE 11-7. *The Control Panel window contains the Desktop icon.*

Wallpaper

Wallpaper is a decorative design displayed on the screen as a background behind windows and icons. Windows provides a choice of 19 wallpaper designs or *(None)*. You can see the list of wallpaper designs in the Desktop dialog box, which is shown in Figure 11-8.

In the bordered area labeled *Wallpaper* you'll see a File drop-down list box. Click the down arrow to see the list of files. Each one is a design that you can choose to be your wallpaper. Select one, but before you choose OK to leave the dialog box, notice the two option buttons: Center and Tile. Be sure that Tile is selected. This will cause your wallpaper design to be repeated until it covers the entire screen instead of just being displayed once in a box in the center. Now choose the OK button. The Argyle wallpaper design (ARGYLE.BMP) is shown in Figure 11-9.

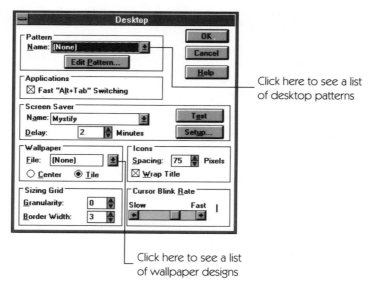

Click here to see a list
of desktop patterns

Click here to see a list
of wallpaper designs

FIGURE 11-8. *The Desktop dialog box.*

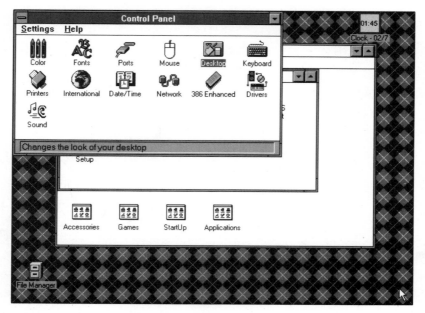

FIGURE 11-9. *The Argyle wallpaper design.*

Making Custom Wallpaper

In Chapter 7, "Working in an Application," you had some experience with Paintbrush. Any Paintbrush painting you create can be used as a wallpaper design in Windows. Save the painting as a bitmap file by choosing 16 Color bitmap (*.BMP) *from the Save File as Type drop-down list box in the Save As dialog box. Be sure to save the painting in your Windows directory. The next time you open Control Panel and double-click the Desktop icon, the filename of your painting will appear in the File drop-down list box for Wallpaper.*

Desktop Pattern

Before you added wallpaper, the screen background was a solid color (by default, light gray). If you set up your wallpaper with the Center option, you still see that solid background color around the edges. You can add a pattern to the solid color. Windows provides 13 desktop patterns. They are accessible in the Desktop dialog box, which you also used to choose wallpaper (Figure 11-8). At the top of the dialog box, in the bordered area labeled *Pattern*, you'll see a Name drop-down list box. Click the down arrow to see the list of pattern names.

Select a pattern. Don't forget to change your wallpaper file to *(None)* or your wallpaper option to Center before you close the dialog box. If a wallpaper design is chosen and the Tile option is selected, the desktop pattern will appear only in the labels of icons. Choose OK to close the Desktop dialog box and to display the background pattern on the screen. As an example, Figure 11-10 shows you the Waffle desktop pattern.

Coloring Your World

On color monitors, Windows displays various parts of the screen in various colors, in a coordinated color scheme. You can pick another color scheme from a list of 23. To see the list of color schemes, start Control Panel and then double-click the Color icon. See Figure 11-11.

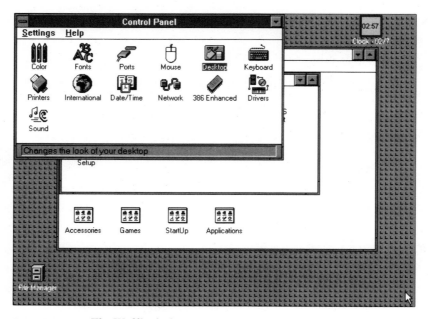

FIGURE 11-10. *The Waffle desktop pattern.*

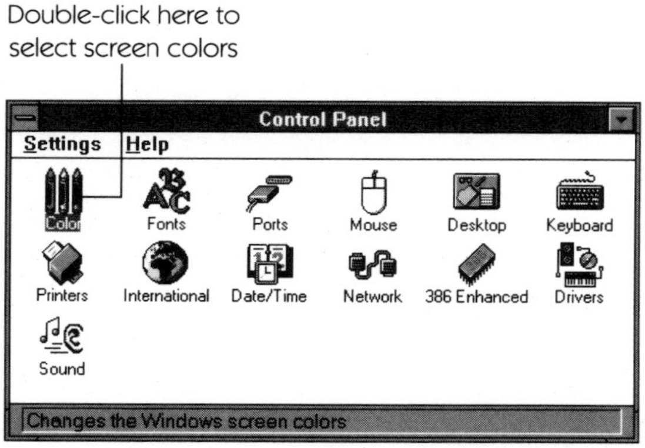

Double-click here to
select screen colors

FIGURE 11-11. *The Control Panel window contains the Color icon.*

The Color dialog box is shown in Figure 11-12. If you click the arrow to
open the drop-down list, you can then use the arrow keys on your keyboard to
move the highlight up and down the list. As each color-scheme name is highlighted, you'll see a small sample of the scheme within the dialog box. Choose

OK when you have highlighted the color scheme you want. In Chapter 15, "Control Panel Revisited," you'll learn how to modify an existing color scheme to create your own color mix.

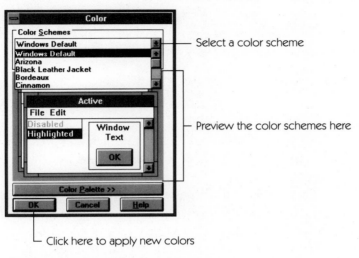

Select a color scheme

Preview the color schemes here

Click here to apply new colors

FIGURE 11-12. *The Color dialog box.*

 Choosing a Color Scheme for LCD Overlay Monitors

More and more people use computers to display visual materials during a presentation. One way to display the computer screen is with an LCD overlay monitor. This device sits on the bed of an overhead projector, which projects the image from the LCD overlay monitor onto a screen where everyone in the room can see the images. One difficulty with this method of projecting presentation images is that the LCD overlay monitor uses various shades of gray in place of colors. The color scheme of the computer must be set up correctly. The three LCD color scheme options in the Color Schemes list (LCD Default Screen Settings, LCD Reversed-Dark, and LCD Reversed-Light) give you three preset color schemes that can make your presentation image clear through an LCD overlay monitor. Try out each LCD color scheme to determine which best meets your presentation needs.

Saving the Screen and Enjoying It Too

The typical computer screen uses a cathode-ray tube (or CRT, a television-like screen) to project images. These screens have a habit of "burning in" an image that is continually displayed for a long time. That is, you will see the burned-in image even when the computer isn't displaying it. It is wise to vary the screen image, especially when you are away from your computer for a period of time. (Turning off the monitor is another way to prevent the burning in of images.)

Screen savers automatically vary your screen image by replacing it with enjoyable animations. The animations take over the screen when you haven't typed on the keyboard or moved the mouse in a while. The additional advantage of screen savers is that the animated image hides your work when you are away from your desk.

Windows provides screen savers that you can activate through the Desktop option of the Control Panel. Open the Control Panel window and double-click the Desktop icon. (See Figure 11-7.) In the Desktop dialog box, you'll see a bordered area labeled *Screen Saver* and inside it a Name drop-down list box. Click the arrow to open the drop-down list, as shown in Figure 11-13.

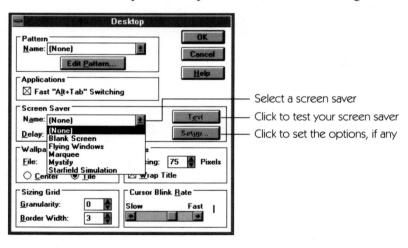

FIGURE 11-13. *The list of Windows screen savers.*

Windows comes with five screen savers. The Marquee screen saver scrolls text across the screen horizontally. Mystify displays dancing colored lines in polygon shapes. Starfield Simulation moves starlike points of light from the middle to the edges of the screen, as if you are traveling very fast through outer space. Flying Windows is similar, but instead of points of light, you see logos of the Windows operating system.

Select a screen saver and then choose the Setup button to set the options, if any, for your choice. As an example, if you select the Marquee screen saver, you can choose Setup in order to type in and format your own Marquee message. The Marquee Setup dialog box is shown in Figure 11-14. You can also select background color, speed, and position of your marquee from among several choices.

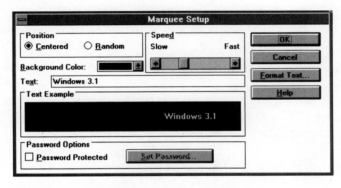

FIGURE 11-14. *The Marquee Setup dialog box.*

When you're done setting screen-saver options and have returned to the Desktop dialog box (Figure 11-13), choose the Test button to see what your screen saver will look like. To stop the test, press any key, move the mouse, or click a mouse button. The Delay text box sets the number of minutes of inaction on your part (no keystrokes, no mouse movements, no mouse clicks) before the screen saver takes over. If you set the delay time to zero, the screen saver never takes over the screen. If a screen saver does take over the screen, just press a key, move the mouse, or click a mouse button to recover your Windows screen.

Setting a Screen Saver Password

Setting a password prevents others from viewing your work after the screen saver has taken over the screen. With password protection, when you press a key or move the mouse, Windows asks for the password. If the password is correct, Windows displays your work screen. If not, Windows resumes the screen saver display.

To set a password, choose the Setup button after selecting a screen saver. Figure 11-14 gives you an example of a Setup dialog box. Turn on the Password Protected check box. (A check box is turned on when it has an X in it, and it's turned off when it's blank. You can turn this check box on or off by clicking the box with the mouse or by pressing Alt+P.) Choose the Set Password button. You will now see the Change Password dialog box, as shown in the picture below. Type your password twice, once in the New Password text box and once in the Retype New Password text box. To turn off password protection, turn off the Password Protected check box.

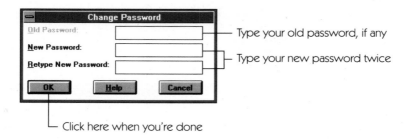

KEEPING YOUR CALENDAR

For all of us, one of our most important assets is our time. For people who attend meetings and for people who must be on schedule, the calendar is a central tool for organizing the day, the week, the month, and the year. The application called Calendar gives you an electronic calendar for recording meetings, setting reminders to leave for meetings, and recording notes about meetings and work.

Start Calendar by double-clicking its icon in the Accessories group window. Figure 11-15 shows a sample Calendar window.

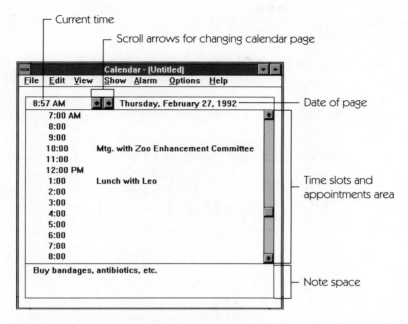

FIGURE 11-15. *The Calendar window.*

Setting Appointments

To make note of an appointment in Calendar, scroll to the date of the appointment (click the scroll arrows at the top of the window or press the Ctrl+Pg Dn or Ctrl+Pg Up key combinations). Click the time slot or press the up or down arrow key to move the blinking vertical line (the insertion point) to the time slot. Type the meeting information.

Setting Off Alarms

Calendar can remind you when it's time to leave for a meeting or appointment. To set an alarm for an appointment, first move the blinking vertical line to the time slot of the appointment and then choose the Set command from the Alarm menu (Alt,A,S or F5). You'll see a little bell icon next to the time, as shown in Figure 11-16. Just as you must keep your alarm clock plugged in for it to work, you must keep Calendar running for it to sound the alarm. After you set the alarm, you can either minimize Calendar's window or leave it the way it is.

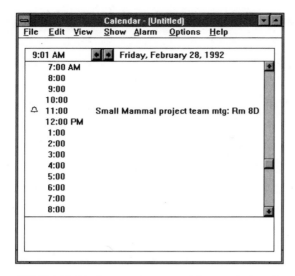

FIGURE 11-16. *An appointment with a reminder alarm set.*

When the appointed time arrives, Calendar beeps four times. If the window isn't minimized, Calendar displays a reminder message right away. See Figure 11-17 for an example. If the window is minimized, the Calendar icon blinks. When you click the blinking icon, Calendar displays the reminder message. Choose OK to close the reminder message box; then head off to your meeting.

FIGURE 11-17. *A reminder message from Calendar.*

Making Notes

To make notes in the space at the bottom of each day's appointments list, click in the note space or press the Tab key so that the blinking vertical line appears in the space. Type your notes. To return to the appointments area, click in the appointments area or press the Tab key again.

Embossing the Calendar with Your Name

Personal desk calendars often have the owner's name embossed on the cover. You can personalize Calendar's display by saving your calendar with your name. Open the File menu and choose the Save command (Alt,F,S). The first time you save a calendar file, you see the Save As dialog box. Type your name in eight or fewer letters. Calendar will automatically add the extension .CAL to the name. (See the section in Chapter 7 called "Saving Files and Opening Files" for more information about file naming.)

In addition to your personal calendar, you might keep separate calendar files for various groups to which you belong. For example, if you belong to a dog club, you could keep a calendar of dog-related events in a calendar file named BRITTANY.CAL.

Chapter 21, "Keeping Up to Date with Calendar," contains more details about using Calendar.

COLLECTING BUSINESS CARDS

In modern business and professional practice, people trade business cards. They put other people's business cards in a file on their desks so that they can quickly locate a particular phone number or address. The application called Cardfile gives you electronic storage for all those cards. You can let Cardfile find the card you need. (You can even have the card dial the phone for you — you will learn about this in Chapter 22.)

Start Cardfile from the Accessories group window. The Cardfile window is shown in Figure 11-18.

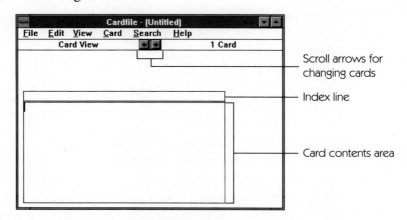

FIGURE 11-18. *The Cardfile window.*

The first time you start Cardfile, you'll see one empty card. After you add cards, you'll see numerous cards and their contents. Cardfile alphabetizes the cards by index line. Figure 11-19 shows Cardfile with several cards; notice the alphabetical arrangement.

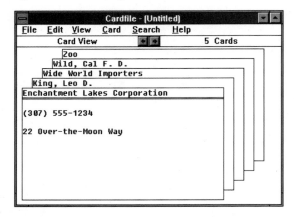

FIGURE 11-19. *A Cardfile window with several cards.*

Recording Names, Addresses, and Phone Numbers

To record a name, address, and phone number in a card, type the information in the card contents area.

To add text to the index line, double-click in that area or choose the Index command from the Edit menu (Alt,E,I or F6). A dialog box appears, as shown in Figure 11-20. Type the text you want in the text box and then choose OK.

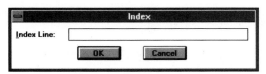

FIGURE 11-20. *The Index dialog box.*

Adding a Card

To add a card to your file, choose the Add command from the Card menu (Alt,C,A or F7). You'll see the dialog box in Figure 11-21.

FIGURE 11-21. *The Add dialog box.*

This dialog box looks like the Index dialog box. In fact, the text you type in the Add text box becomes the index line of a new card.

Finding a Particular Card

If the card you want is visible in the window, you can click in the card to bring it to the front. You can also click the scroll arrows at the top of the window or press the Pg Up and Pg Dn keys to scroll through the cards.

You can also use the Go To command on the Search menu to find the next card with specific text in its index line. The text you type in the Go To text box can be any series of characters that appear in the index line. For example, to find a card that shows *Leo* in its index line, you would choose the Go To command (Alt,S,G or F4), type *Leo* in the Go To text box, and choose OK. See Figure 11-22. After you choose OK, the card with *Leo* in its index line will be brought to the front of the card stack.

FIGURE 11-22. *The Go To dialog box.*

Chapter 22, ''Keeping Tabs on Business Contacts in Cardfile,'' describes how to use the Find command to find text in a card's contents area.

Saving Cards

To save your cards for ready use, choose the Save command from the File menu (Alt,F,S). The first time you save a file, you'll see the Save As dialog box. You must give your file a name of no more than eight letters. Cardfile will automatically add the extension .CRD. (See the section in Chapter 7 called ''Saving Files and Opening Files'' to learn about file naming.)

Chapter 12

Printing Your Work

Unless your company really has established the paperless office, you'll need to print your work. All printing in the Windows operating system is centralized; you just have to install your printer in Windows. (You probably did this during Windows Setup, but if you didn't, you'll get another chance soon.) This chapter first tells how to install and choose a printer and then goes on to describe the three major ways to print your work.

STARTING THE PRESSES (PRINTER SETUP)

During Windows Setup, you were shown a dialog box in which you could select your printer. If you didn't install your printer during the setup process, maybe someone else did. How can you find out? You find out by checking in the Printers dialog box, as described below. If you learn that you don't have a printer installed, you can install it now. Also, if you got a new printer since installing Windows, you'll want to install your new printer. You need to start Control Panel from the Main group window of Program Manager. The Control Panel window is shown in Figure 12-1.

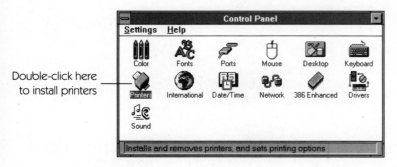

Double-click here to install printers

FIGURE 12-1. *The Control Panel window contains the Printers icon.*

Installing a Printer from Control Panel

In the Control Panel window, double-click the Printers icon. You'll see the Printers dialog box shown in Figure 12-2. You can see if your current printer is in the Installed Printers list box.

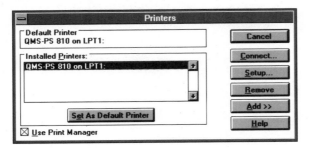

FIGURE 12-2. *The Printers dialog box.*

If your printer is already installed, skip down to the section "Setting Up a Printer" below. If you need to install another printer, choose the Add button in the Printers dialog box. The dialog box will change to look like Figure 12-3.

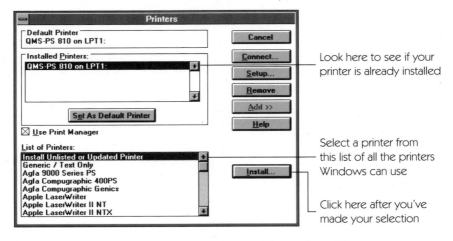

Look here to see if your printer is already installed

Select a printer from this list of all the printers Windows can use

Click here after you've made your selection

FIGURE 12-3. *The Printers dialog box after you choose the Add button.*

When you select a new printer from the list of printers, choose the Install button. If the printer you selected is similar to a printer you have already installed, Windows simply adds the name to the Installed Printers list box. If the new printer is different from all the printers you have installed, Windows asks you to insert the floppy disk that contains a file Windows needs before it can use the selected printer. An example of the message box is shown in Figure 12-4. Windows asks for a file called HPPCL.DRV.

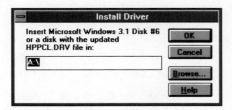

FIGURE 12-4. *An example of the Install Driver message box.*

If you see the message box, insert the requested disk. If you insert the disk in a disk drive other than A, type the disk drive letter in the text box before choosing OK. You will then see the new printer name in the Installed Printers list box. After the printer is installed, check that its setup is correct.

Setting up a printer

To check the setup of an installed printer, select the printer from the Installed Printers list box in the Printers dialog box (Figure 12-2). Then choose the Setup button. Different printers offer different setup options. For an HP Laser-Jet Series II printer, you see the dialog box shown in Figure 12-5.

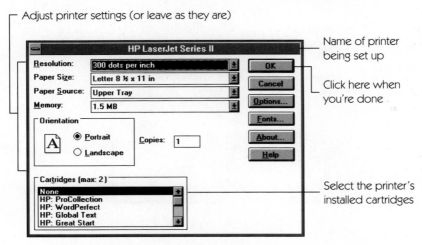

FIGURE 12-5. *The setup dialog box for an HP LaserJet Series II printer.*

If you're unsure which printer settings to select, you can leave the settings as they are. Be sure to select the cartridges you have installed in the printer so that Windows can use the fonts available in the cartridges. After you choose the OK button, Windows returns you to the Printers dialog box.

Choosing a different default printer

Unless you specify otherwise, when you print your work, Windows uses the printer designated as the default printer in the Printers dialog box of Control Panel (Figure 12-2). If you need to change the default printer, select the new default printer from the Installed Printers list and then choose the button Set As Default Printer. The selected printer's name now appears in the Default Printer section of the Printers dialog box.

Setting Up and Choosing a Printer from Inside an Application

Within most applications for Windows, you'll find a Print Setup command on the File menu. This command gives you a handy way to change a printer's setup options. It also enables you to print with an installed printer other than the default printer.

Because the Print Setup command is a standard part of Windows, you will always know which command to choose to change printing options. You can start any application that's included with Windows, such as Paintbrush, and choose the Print Setup command from the File menu (Alt,F,R) to select a different printer from the default. See Figure 12-6.

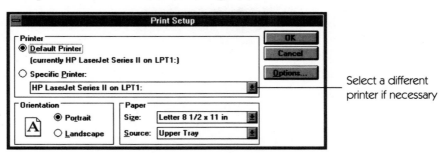

FIGURE 12-6. *The Print Setup dialog box in Paintbrush.*

114

PRINTING FROM AN APPLICATION

Most of the time you'll probably want to print your work from within the application that you used to create the work. Every application in Windows that has something to print has the standard Print command on its File menu. The contents of the Print dialog box changes from application to application because each tool needs its own specific printing information. In Cardfile, the Print command has no dialog box. Cardfile simply displays a message box that lets you know the cards are being printed. In Calendar, the Print dialog box asks only for the dates you want printed. The Print dialog box in Paintbrush requests more information, as shown in Figure 12-7.

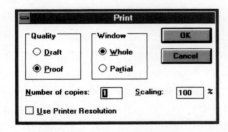

FIGURE 12-7. *The Print dialog box in Paintbrush.*

PRINTING WITHIN FILE MANAGER

At times you might need to print your work when the application you used to create the work isn't running. Rather than starting the application, opening the work file, and then printing, you can sometimes print directly from within File Manager—a shortcut that is very convenient.

To print within File Manager, select the file you want to print and then choose the Print command from the File menu (Alt,F,P). Windows inserts the file's name in the Print text box, as shown in Figure 12-8. There are some restrictions on the types of files you can print from File Manager. You can

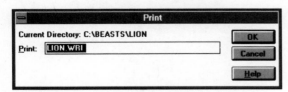

FIGURE 12-8. *The Print dialog box in File Manager.*

only print files created in the applications found in the Accessories group window (applications like Paintbrush, Notepad, Calendar, and Write).

When you choose the Print command in File Manager, File Manager starts the application you used to create the file and then chooses the Print command from the File menu in that tool. If the application's Print command has a dialog box, you see the dialog box. You can change any printing instructions, as necessary, and then choose OK to start printing. When printing is finished, File Manager quits the application for you.

PRINTING BY DRAGGING FILES FROM FILE MANAGER TO PRINT MANAGER

In Chapter 16 you'll learn about Print Manager and how to use it to control your printing. Right now, you'll learn how to use Print Manager with File Manager to print your work. This technique can only be used to print files created in the applications found in the Accessories group window.

You start Print Manager as you start all applications in Windows. The Print Manager's icon is found in the Main group window of Program Manager. After you start Print Manager by double-clicking the icon, you can leave Print Manager as a restored window on your screen or minimize it to an application icon. The icon is handier because it takes up less space on the screen and is easier to see with the File Manager window restored.

When Print Manager is running, open File Manager. Locate the file you want to print. Then drag the file's icon to the Print Manager window or to Print Manager's icon. The file's icon will contain a plus sign when it is on top of Print Manager's window or icon. Release the mouse button to start printing. Just as File Manager did when you chose the Print command, Print Manager opens the Print dialog box if there is one. You change any printing instructions, as necessary, in the dialog box and then choose OK to start printing. When printing is finished, Print Manager quits the application for you.

Part Two

Windows in More Depth

Having mastered the basic skills, you're ready for Part Two, which will teach you more about the powerful core applications in the Windows operating system.

Chapter 13

More About Program Manager

Chapter 3 ("Starting Out, Finding Your Way, and Quitting") introduced you to the basics of Program Manager in the Windows operating system. There you learned about the Program Manager group windows that contain icons for applications. These icons make it easy to start an application without having to remember where on your computer's hard disk the application file is stored.

In this chapter you'll learn more about using Program Manager. Most of what you learn will help you set up Program Manager to make it easier to start programs. Among other things, you'll learn how to

- Start an application that doesn't have an icon in a group window
- Minimize the Program Manager window when you start an application
- Add, move, and delete an icon in a group window
- Change which program an icon starts and change the icon graphic
- Start applications automatically when you start Windows
- Add, rename, and delete a group window

STARTING APPLICATIONS WITHOUT ICONS

The icons in Program Manager's group windows provide a convenient way to start your most frequently used applications. For applications you rarely use, you might choose not to create an icon in order to keep the number of icons in Program Manager manageable and to avoid visual clutter. In particular, you might leave out some non-Windows applications. To run applications that don't have an icon in a group window, choose the Run command from the File menu (Alt,F,R). The dialog box is shown in Figure 13-1. Use the Browse button to enter a *command line* for you in the Command Line text box.

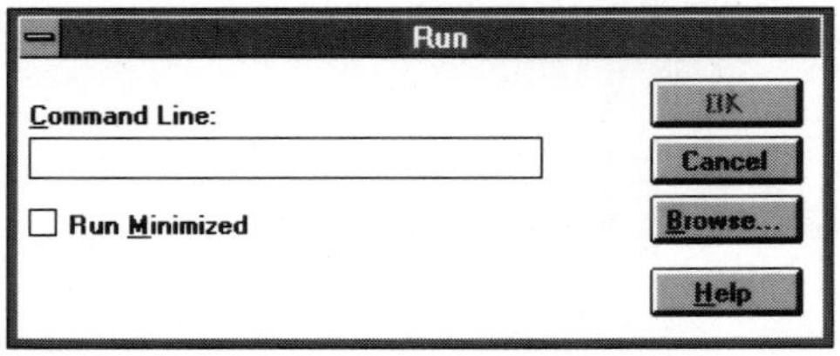

FIGURE 13-1. *The Run dialog box.*

At a minimum, a command line will require the name of the application's program file. If the program file you want (usually a file with .EXE at the end of its name) isn't in the Windows directory, you must add a *path* in front of the name of the program file to tell Windows where on your hard disk the program file can be found. Windows can help you create a path, if you choose the Browse button in the Run dialog box. Figure 13-2 shows the Browse dialog box. You'll need to double-click the folder icons until you get to the location of the program file you want to run. Then, if you double-click the filename, Windows will close the Browse dialog box and write the correct path and filename in the Command Line text box. See Figure 13-3. When you choose OK in the Run dialog box, Windows starts the program.

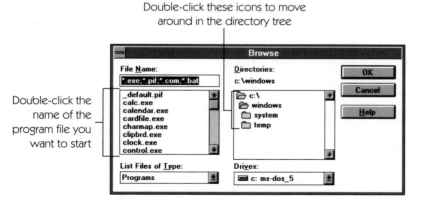

FIGURE 13-2. *The Browse dialog box.*

Path and filename appear here after
you double-click the name of a
program file in the Browse dialog box

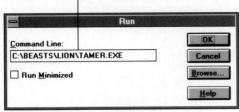

FIGURE 13-3. *The Run dialog box with a program file's path and name in the Command Line text box.*

EXERCISING YOUR OPTIONS

Program Manager gives you several options that can help you keep your work space well organized. You can set an option to minimize Program Manager when you start an application. You can also set an option to automatically clean up the display of icons in group windows.

Minimizing Program Manager Automatically

As originally set up, Program Manager retains its current size when you start an application. Minimizing Program Manager when you run an application saves computer memory, keeps the screen from becoming cluttered, and makes it easy to switch to Program Manager by double-clicking its icon. To minimize Program Manager automatically when you start an application, choose the Minimize on Use command from the Options menu (Alt,O,M).

Keeping Icons Tidy

In Chapter 8, "Arranging Icons and Windows," you saw the effect of changing the size of a group window. You then learned how to use the Arrange Icons command on the Window menu to arrange the icons so that the horizontal scroll bar is eliminated. When you start adding icons to a group window, the arrangement might become disorderly. The Arrange Icons command (Alt,W,A) straightens up the display of icons. If you often find yourself using the Arrange Icons command, you can turn on the option to have Program Manager automatically arrange icons.

Choose the Auto Arrange command from the Options menu (Alt,O,A) to tell Program Manager to rearrange icons in all group windows whenever you change the size of a group window, modify its contents, or use the Cascade command or Tile command from the Window menu.

ACCESSING GROUP WINDOWS FROM A MENU

Because you can move the group windows around within the Program Manager window and change their sizes, some windows and icons can get covered up, making them inaccessible to the mouse. To display a group window that is obscured, you can use Ctrl+Tab to move to any of the group windows or icons, as explained in Chapter 3, "Starting Out, Finding Your Way, and Quitting." Another, simpler, way is to open the Window menu and choose the window you'd like to see from the list at the bottom of the menu, as shown in Figure 13-4. Notice that the name of the currently active group window has a check mark next to it. With the keyboard, press the key for the number beside the group window's name.

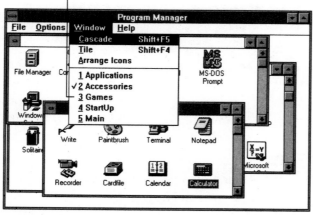

FIGURE 13-4. *The Window menu in Program Manager.*

ADDING AN ICON TO A GROUP WINDOW

You might have an application on your computer that doesn't have an icon in Program Manager. You can easily add an icon for this application to any group window.

First, the group window to which you want to add the icon should be the active window. Next, you need to open the File menu and choose the New command (Alt,F,N). The New Program Object dialog box appears. The Program Item button should be selected, as shown in Figure 13-5. Choose OK.

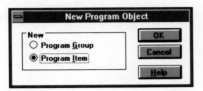

FIGURE 13-5. *The New Program Object dialog box.*

When you choose OK, Windows displays the Program Item Properties dialog box, shown in Figure 13-6. In the Description text box, type the label you want to be displayed under the icon. In the Command Line text box, you'll have to type, at a minimum, the name of the application's program file (usually a name that ends in .EXE), and you'll probably have to write the full path to tell Windows where the file is located. You can use the Browse button to help you out here. The process of using the Browse dialog box to select a program file is explained at the beginning of this chapter, in the section called "Starting Applications Without Icons."

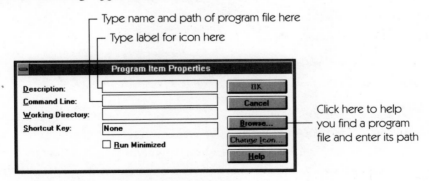

FIGURE 13-6. *The Program Item Properties dialog box.*

After you choose the OK button in the Program Item Properties dialog box, you can immediately use the new icon to start the application in the same way you use any other application icon. If you left the Description text box blank, Windows uses the program filename (without the .EXE extension) as the icon label.

Starting an Application in the Minimized State

If you want Windows to start an application in the minimized state when it's started from Program Manager, turn on the Run Minimized check box in the Program Item Properties dialog box (Figure 13-6). To start the application as a window, leave the check box turned off.

SURVEYING ICON PROPERTIES

After you set up an icon, you might want to change its label or add *switches* (special instructions) to the command line. To make these changes, click the icon so that its label is highlighted and then choose the Properties command from the File menu (Alt,F,P or Alt+Enter). You see the same dialog box you saw when you created a new icon, the Program Item Properties dialog box, except that the text boxes are filled in. See Figure 13-7.

FIGURE 13-7. *A Program Item Properties dialog box for a selected icon.*

To change the icon's label, type a new label in the Description text box. To add switches to the command line, type them in the Command Line text box after the path. (You'll have to read an application's documentation to know what switches are possible here.) Choose the OK button to make the changes to the icon.

Opening a Specific Work File with an Icon

Normally Windows starts applications with new, untitled, blank pages. With the Properties command on the File menu, you can set up an application so that it starts a specific work file. All you have to do is replace the program name (for example, CALENDAR.EXE) with the name of the file you want to start (for example, RUSSB.CAL) in the Program Item Properties dialog box, as shown below.

Program Item Properties	
Description: `Calendar`	OK
Command Line: `RUSSB.CAL`	Cancel
Working Directory: ` `	
Shortcut Key: `None`	Browse...
☐ **R**un Minimized	Change Icon...
	Help

In addition to changing an icon's label and command-line information, you can also change the icon graphic for any application. Even if the manufacturer of an application supplied only one icon graphic, you can choose a different one.

Try changing an icon now by clicking the Paintbrush icon (in the Accessories group window) so that the icon's label is highlighted. Then choose the Properties command. Windows inserts the name of Paintbrush's program file and its description in the Command Line and Description text boxes. You also have a view of Paintbrush's current icon.

Next, choose the Change Icon button. To see many different icons, choose the Browse button from inside the Change Icon dialog box and select *PROGMAN.EXE* from the File Name list box. (Be sure you are looking in the Windows directory of your hard disk.) Once you have selected PROGMAN.EXE, choose OK in the Browse dialog box. This brings you back to the Change Icon dialog box. Scroll to see the list of icons that the PROGMAN.EXE program file offers, as shown in Figure 13-8, and double-click one to choose it. This icon will become your new icon for Paintbrush.

Choose OK in the Program Item Properties dialog box. The new icon now appears in its group window.

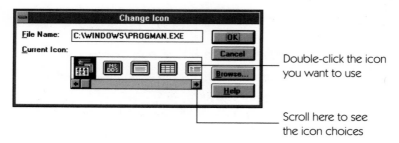

Double-click the icon
you want to use

Scroll here to see
the icon choices

FIGURE 13-8. *The Change Icon dialog box with icon choices from PROGMAN.EXE.*

Finding Icons for Popular Applications

Windows installs a file named MORICONS.DLL, which contains icons for many popular applications. This file is designed to give you product-specific icons for non-Windows versions of various applications. To see the icons, use the same steps you used in the "Surveying Icon Properties" section to see the icons in PROGMAN.EXE.

MOVING AN ICON TO A DIFFERENT GROUP

When you install a new application for Windows, that application's setup program might create a new group window, one you don't want. Windows allows you to move the application's icon to any existing group window. (Later you'll learn how to add new group windows and delete others.)

To move an icon from one group window to another with the mouse, drag the icon to the new group window. To move an icon with the keyboard, select the icon and choose the Move command from the File menu (Alt,F,M or F7). You must specify in the Move Program Item dialog box the group window to which you want to move the icon.

DELETING ICONS

Some icons become obsolete when you install a replacement application or change your work habits. To save space in a group window, you can delete icons you no longer need or want.

To delete an icon in a group window, click the icon to select it and choose the Delete command from the File menu (Alt,F,D or Del). Program Manager displays a message box asking whether you really want to delete the icon (Figure 13-9).

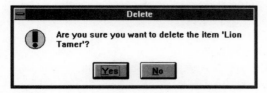

FIGURE 13-9. *The Delete message box.*

You can add the icon to a group window in Program Manager again at any time, using the procedure discussed previously.

ADDING A GROUP WINDOW

If you decide that you'd like to add a group window to Program Manager, choose the New command from the File menu (Alt,F,N). Choose the Program Group button instead of the Program Item button (Figure 13-10). The Program Group Properties dialog box will appear, as shown in Figure 13-11.

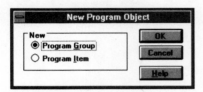

FIGURE 13-10. *The New Program Object dialog box with the Program Group button selected.*

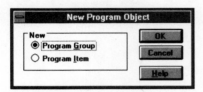

FIGURE 13-11. *The Program Group Properties dialog box.*

In the Description text box in the dialog box, type a name for your new group window. Leave the Group File text box blank; Windows uses the first eight characters of the Description and adds the filename extension .GRP to create a file that contains information about the new group window. When you choose OK, Windows displays the new, empty group window in the Program Manager window, ready for you to add icons.

 Automatically Starting Applications When You Start Windows

If you always start the same applications every time you start Windows, you can set up a special group window, called StartUp. Move the icons of the applications you want to start every time you start Windows to the StartUp group window. In Chapter 11, "Creating Your Own Work Space," you learned about Clock, Calendar, and Cardfile. To automatically set up your desk with these applications when you start Windows, set up your StartUp group window as shown below:

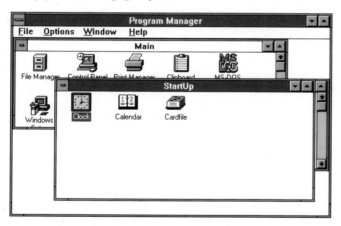

RENAMING OR DELETING A GROUP WINDOW

If you want to change the title of a group window, you must first minimize the group window and then select the minimized group window's icon by pressing the Ctrl+Tab key combination until the icon's label is highlighted. With the minimized group window's icon selected, choose the Properties command from the File menu (Alt,F,P or Alt+Enter). This command displays the same dialog box that you saw when you created a group window. Type the new group window title, and then choose OK.

When you no longer need a group window, move or delete all the icons from the window and then choose the Delete command from the File menu (Alt,F,D or Del). Program Manager will ask you to confirm your intention before deleting the group.

Deleting Icons and Group Window All at Once

If you want to delete a group window and all its icons, minimize the group window and then choose the Delete command from the File menu (Alt,F,D or Del). Program Manager deletes the icons and the window. You will see a message asking for your consent only for the group window, not for the icons in the group.

Chapter 14

More About File Manager

File Manager in the Windows operating system displays the directory structure and contents of drives, as you learned in Chapter 10, ''Managing Files.'' In this chapter you'll discover that File Manager can display information in a variety of ways; for example, File Manager can arrange files according to how big they are or when they were last saved. And a number of important tasks can be accomplished from within File Manager, tasks like creating directories and opening files. In this chapter, you'll learn how to

- Change the order in which files appear in their window panes
- Display additional details about files (beyond their names)
- Limit the list of files to files of a particular type
- Change the format of the text File Manager uses to display file and directory names
- Rename files and directories
- Create directories
- Delete files and directories
- Search for files
- Start applications from within File Manager
- Open files of your work
- Copy disks

SORTING FILES TO YOUR ORDERS

By default, File Manager lists in the directory-contents pane (the pane on the right) the names of files and directories in alphabetic order. But suppose that at the end of the day you want to copy your day's work onto a floppy disk. You want to see and be able to quickly select just the files you worked on today. Alphabetic order doesn't help you in this task.

File Manager provides four commands on its View menu for changing the order in which directories and files appear in a directory-contents pane. These commands are listed and described in Figure 14-1. Note that File Manager always lists the directories first, followed by the files. Directories and files are sorted separately.

View Menu Command	Effect on Order of List
Sort By Name	Lists directories and then files in alphabetic order
Sort By Type	Lists directories alphabetically and then files by file extension
Sort By Size	Lists directories alphabetically and then files by file size, largest file at the top of the list
Sort By Date	Lists directories and then files by the date they were last saved, most recent date at the top of the list

FIGURE 14-1. *The effect of Sort commands on the list of files and directories in a directory-contents pane.*

EXPANDING FILE INFORMATION

As mentioned above, the File Manager directory-contents pane initially lists only the names of files and directories. Sometimes you want to know more about a file. File Manager can also display the dates and times the directories were created, the sizes of the files, the dates and times the files were last saved (or were created if they've never been changed), and the attributes of the files. The View menu contains three commands for changing the amount of file details you see. They are listed and explained in Figure 14-2.

View Menu Command	Effect on Details in List
Name	Lists only names of directories and files
All File Details	Lists names of directories, and the dates and times they were created; lists names of files, their sizes, the dates and times they were last saved, and their file attributes
Partial Details	Lists details of directories and files as selected in the Partial Details dialog box

FIGURE 14-2. *The effect of Name and Details commands on the list in a directory-contents pane.*

To select only the file details you want to appear in the directory-contents panes, choose the Partial Details command from the View menu (Alt,V,P). Use the check boxes in the Partial Details dialog box, as shown in Figure 14-3.

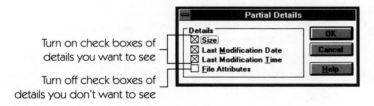

Turn on check boxes of details you want to see

Turn off check boxes of details you don't want to see

FIGURE 14-3. *The Partial Details dialog box.*

SEEING ONLY THE FILES YOU WANT TO SEE

Finding a particular file in a long list can be tedious. You might want to reduce the list of filenames to include only files of a particular type. A reduced list can also make it easy to quickly select files for copying or deletion. On the View menu, File Manager has a By File Type command. Choose this command (Alt,V,T) to display the By File Type dialog box (shown in Figure 14-4), with which you can add or remove types of files from the lists in the directory-contents panes. The dialog box contains five check boxes. Figure 14-5 describes the results of turning on each of these check boxes.

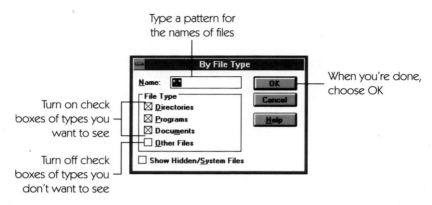

FIGURE 14-4. *The By File Type dialog box.*

By File Type Check Box	Effect on Items in List
Directories	Lists directories
Programs	Lists files with the extensions .BAT, .COM, .EXE, and .PIF
Documents	Lists files that contain data (your work files)
Other Files	Lists files that don't fit the other three categories
Show Hidden/ System Files	Lists files that have the hidden file or system file attribute assigned and that are of the type specified by the other check boxes that have been turned on

FIGURE 14-5. *The effect of By File Type check boxes on the list in a directory-contents pane.*

At the top of the By File Type dialog box, you see the Name text box. This text box, which names the files to be listed, usually contains the characters *.*. An asterisk in the name of a file means any combination of characters up to the maximum length. Because the names of files can contain up to eight characters followed by a period followed by up to three characters (the extension), the first asterisk means any combination of characters in any number from one through eight. The second asterisk means any combination of characters in any number from none through three. (You can omit the characters after the period.) By this logic, the characters *.* in the Name text box mean that every file of the types checked below will be listed.

You can narrow the list of files further by typing more specific characters in the Name text box. The most specific list would be the name of a specific file. To see a list of files with a specific extension, type * followed by the extension. For example, to see only files created by the Calendar application, type *.cal. You can also type part of the name of a file and follow it with an asterisk. For example, suppose you start the filename of every letter you write with the letters *ltr* and all your letters have the extension .WRI (because you write your letters in the Write application for Windows). To see a list of only your letters, type *ltr*.wri* in the Name text box.

The asterisk is called a *wildcard character*. Like wild cards in a card game, a wildcard character can represent any character at all. As mentioned, the asterisk means any number of characters. When you want to use a wildcard character to indicate only a single character, you use the question mark. For example, suppose that you have files with names that start with *gsw* followed by additional characters. Some of these files have two numbers following *gsw* in their names. Other files have more or fewer characters after *gsw*. To list only the files that begin with *gsw* followed by two characters, you type *gsw??.**.

Remember that when you type something in the Name text box of the By File Type dialog box, you are asking the File Manager to list only files that fit that pattern and that also belong in the categories you have checked in the File Type section of the dialog box. As an example, suppose you type *ltr*.wri* in the Name text box. Suppose also that you have only letters (document files) and no directories with that name. If the Documents check box is not checked, the directory-contents pane of File Manager will be empty in every directory!

CHANGING TEXT

File Manager displays the names of directories, the names of files, drive letters, and disk labels in all lowercase letters. File Manager uses the MS Sans Serif font in 8-point size. You can change the font, font style, font size, and case of the names. Open the Options menu and choose the Font command (Alt,O,F). File Manager displays the Font dialog box shown in Figure 14-6. Now make any change that you want. Notice that the box labeled *Sample* shows you how the text will look. When you've finished making changes, choose OK.

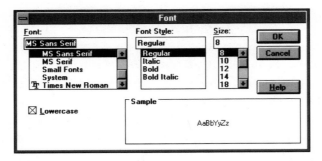

FIGURE 14-6. *The Font dialog box.*

RENAMING FILES AND DIRECTORIES

File Manager makes it easy to change the name of a file or directory. To change a name, select the file or directory, open the File menu and choose the Rename command (Alt,F,N). Then type the new name in the text box labeled *To*, as shown in Figure 14-7.

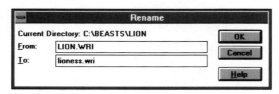

FIGURE 14-7. *The Rename dialog box for a file.*

NOTE *Some applications for Windows keep a list of the last few files you worked on. If you change the name of one of these files, you might see a message when you try to use the application that the file cannot be found. Don't worry. Choose the Open command from the File menu to open the file with its new name.*

CREATING A NEW DIRECTORY

When you need to add another directory to a disk, activate the disk drive by clicking its icon in File Manager, and then select the directory into which you want to add a directory. Choose the Create Directory command from the File menu (Alt,F,E). Now type the name of the new directory in the Create Directory dialog box (shown in Figure 14-8).

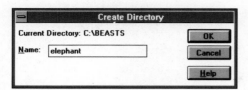

FIGURE 14-8. *The Create Directory dialog box.*

DELETING FILES AND DIRECTORIES

You can delete any file or directory on a disk. To delete a file, select it and choose the Delete command from the File menu (Alt,F,D or Del). To delete a directory, select the directory either in the directory-tree pane or in the directory-contents pane and then choose the Delete command (Alt,F,D or Del). File Manager asks whether you *really* want to delete the directory. Then File Manager asks whether you *really* want to delete each file in the directory. Luckily, you can choose the Yes to All button when File Manager asks about the first file. That way, File Manager won't bug you before deleting each and every file. Of course, if you want to be asked about deleting each and every file, choose the Yes (or No) button when the message box appears.

 NOTE *Be careful about deleting files and directories for applications that are running. If you delete a file the application needs, you might damage other work files. Before you delete files used by an application, quit the application.*

SEARCHING FOR FILES

Sometimes you simply forget where you put a certain file. Looking for the file in every directory can take too long. Even if you go through that exhaustive procedure, you might overlook the one file you want to find. Because hard-disk drives can store many files in many directories, it sometimes seems that a hard-disk drive loves to hide your files. Your answer is the Search command, which you can use to find files, no matter where on a drive they're stored.

To search for a file, open the File menu and choose the Search command (Alt,F,H).

The Search dialog box, shown in Figure 14-9, provides a Search For text box in which you can type a filename, a directory name, or a filename pattern. If you have a file selected when you choose the Search command, File Manager inserts an asterisk followed by a period and the selected file's extension in the Search For text box. For example, if you have the file MOUSE.SYS selected in the directory-contents pane, File Manager inserts *.SYS in the Search For text box. If you have no file selected in the active window, File Manager inserts *.*. You can include wildcard characters in the Search For text box. (Use an asterisk for a series of consecutive characters and a question mark for a single character, as explained in the previous section "Seeing Only the Files You Want to See.")

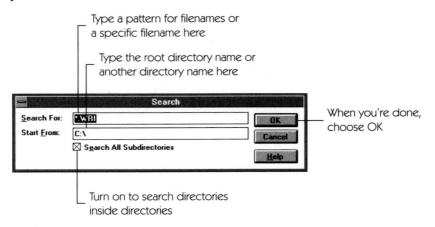

FIGURE 14-9. *The Search dialog box.*

After you choose OK in the Search dialog box, File Manager searches the disk for files and then opens a special window (an example of which is shown in Figure 14-10) that displays the files it found. You can work with the directories and files shown in this Search Results window in the same way you work with them in the directory-contents pane. You can double-click program files and work files in the Search Results window to open them. Double-clicking a program file's name (for example, PBRUSH.EXE) starts the program; double-clicking a work file's name (for example, LION1.BMP) starts the application in which the work file was created and loads the file. In addition, you can copy, delete, and move any directory or file in the Search Results window.

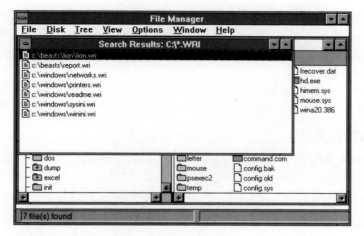

FIGURE 14-10. *A Search Results window.*

Searching an Entire Drive

To search an entire drive, select the icon for the drive's root directory before you choose the Search command. (The root directory is the highest-level directory on a drive; for example, C:\ is the root directory on the C drive.) Then, in the Search dialog box, leave the Search All Subdirectories check box turned on.

If you choose the Search command again to search for other files, File Manager replaces the contents of the Search Results window with the new results. You can have only one Search Results window open at a time.

STARTING SOMETHING

Program Manager is the primary application you use to start other applications in Windows. As you learned in Chapter 13, you can start applications that don't have icons by choosing the Run command from the File menu in Program Manager. An alternative to using Program Manager's Run command is to start applications from File Manager. You can even use File Manager to open a specific work file and start its application at the same time.

Starting an Application

If an application doesn't have an icon set up in Program Manager, you can start that application from a File Manager window. Click the folder of the directory that contains the application's program file, locate the icon for the program file, and then double-click it. See Figure 14-11. (With the keyboard, select the program file and press Enter.)

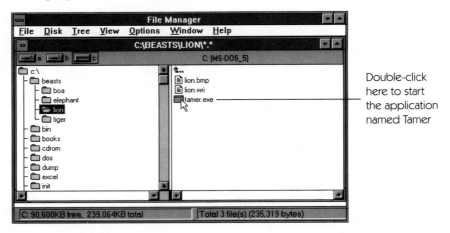

FIGURE 14-11. *Starting an application in File Manager by double-clicking its program file.*

File Manager contains a Run command like Program Manager's. If you first select a program file and then open the File menu and choose Run (Alt,F,R), the application is started when you choose OK. You can also type the program file's name in the Run dialog box.

Opening a File of Your Work

It's often very convenient to open a specific work file as you start an application. File Manager provides several methods to accomplish this task.

To open a specific work file, double-click the file icon. (With the keyboard, you can select the work file and press the Enter key.) A second way to open a work file as you start an application is to select the work file in File Manager, choose the Run command from the File menu and choose OK. With either method you must first associate the work file with its parent application, as explained in the next section.

As an alternative, you can drag the work file and drop it on the program file of the application you used to create the work file. See Figure 14-12. If you drag the work file onto the program file, File Manager displays a message asking you to confirm that you want to start the application and open the selected work file.

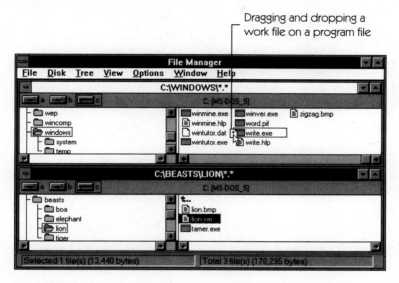

Dragging and dropping a
work file on a program file

FIGURE 14-12. *Starting an application in File Manager by dragging and dropping a work file (LION.WRI) on its program file (WRITE.EXE).*

Associating a File with an Application

Before you can start an application by double-clicking a work file icon, the work file must be associated with that application. Many applications for Windows set up the association when you install the application. (For example, files with the .BMP extension are associated with Paintbrush during the Windows setup process.)

To associate a type of work file with an application, select a work file of the type you want to associate, go to the File menu, and choose the Associate command (Alt,F,A). Then use the Associate dialog box (shown in Figure 14-13) to specify the application that will be associated with that type of file. Note that, when you're done, the association will apply to all files that have the same extension as the work file you selected.

Extension of the selected file

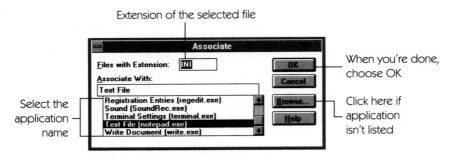

When you're done, choose OK

Select the application name

Click here if application isn't listed

FIGURE 14-13. *The Associate dialog box.*

Adding Icons to Program Manager Group Windows

In Chapter 13, "More About Program Manager," you learned how to add icons to group windows. File Manager gives you an even easier method for adding an icon to a group window in Program Manager.

First, organize your computer screen so that you can see both the group window in Program Manager to which you want to add an icon and the directory-contents pane in File Manager that contains the application's program file. Then drag the program file from File Manager to the Program Manager group window. (See the illustration on the opposite page.) That's all there is to it. There is now an icon for the application in the group window. The icon's label consists of the first eight characters of the file's name (up to the period). You can use Program Manager to survey the icon's properties (as described in Chapter 13 in the section "Surveying Icon Properties") and change them as you wish. Changing the title is one reason to choose the Properties command (Alt,F,P) for the new icon.

You can use this same method to add an icon for a work file to Program Manager. For example, if you drag the file RUSSB.CAL (a personal calendar file) from File Manager to a Program Manager group window, the Calendar icon appears and has the title Russb.

Dragging CALENDAR.EXE from File Manager to
create an icon in the StartUp group window

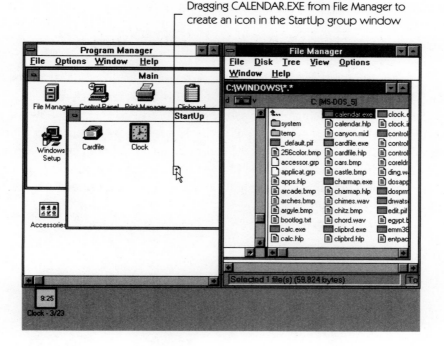

COPYING A DISK

It's important to safeguard the contents of your disks by making backup
copies. You can use File Manager to copy the entire contents of a floppy disk
onto another floppy disk. The Copy Disk command on the Disk menu formats
the destination disk (if it hasn't yet been done) and copies the directories,
files, and disk label from the source disk. As you probably know, you can use
floppy disks of varying capacities with your computer, but you can only use
the Copy Disk command to copy a disk to another disk with the same
capacity.

To copy a floppy disk using Copy Disk, insert the source disk in the drive
you want to copy from and, if you have two floppy-disk drives of the same
capacity, insert the destination disk in the destination drive. Open the Disk

menu and choose the Copy Disk command (Alt,D,C). Select a source and destination drive letter in the dialog box and choose OK. The File Manager displays a message asking you to insert the source disk. After you choose OK, you see a message reporting the progress of copying.

If your source and destination drives are the same, follow the instructions that File Manager displays in message boxes telling you to switch disks. After you switch disks by taking out the source disk, inserting the destination disk, and choosing OK, the copying of files to the destination disk begins. Copying proceeds until File Manager needs the source disk again. If your computer has lots of memory, you might not need to switch disks. If your computer has a small amount of memory, you might be asked to switch the disks several times.

 **Copying Between Disks
of Different Capacities**

You can't use the Copy Disk command to copy a disk onto another disk with a different capacity, but you can still copy information *between these dissimilar disks. Here's how. Click the drive icon of the disk you want to copy. Then select the root directory—the topmost folder in the directory-tree pane—and drag it to the drive icon of the disk drive to which you want to copy the contents.*

Chapter 15

Control Panel Revisited

In Chapter 11, "Creating Your Own Work Space," you used Control Panel to add a wallpaper design to your screen and to pick a desktop pattern. Control Panel is where you go to customize the Windows operating system. In addition to the changes you made with Control Panel in Chapter 11, you can select different colors for various elements in Windows, edit a desktop pattern, set icon labels to appear in one or two lines, change the rate at which the cursor blinks, adjust the operation of the mouse and keyboard, and turn on and off the computer's beep.

SETTING CUSTOM SCREEN COLORS

In Chapter 11 you learned to select a color scheme. Each color scheme is a preset combination of colors for the various elements on the screen in Windows. You can also change the color of individual elements in a color scheme to create your own custom design.

To change the colors of screen elements, start Control Panel from the Main group window in Program Manager, and then double-click the Color icon to bring up the Color dialog box, which is shown in Figure 15-1.

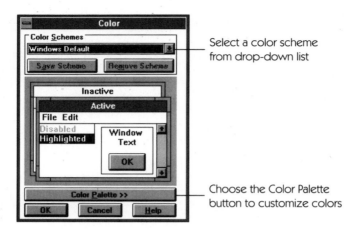

FIGURE 15-1. *The Color dialog box.*

Making a Color Scheme Your Own

Begin creating your own color scheme by choosing the Color Palette button in the Color dialog box. The dialog box will expand, as shown in Figure 15-2.

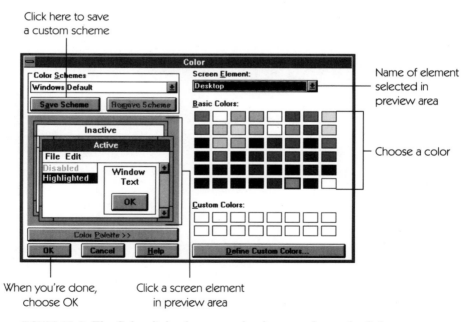

FIGURE 15-2. *The Color dialog box expands when you choose the Color Palette button.*

To change the color of a screen element, either click the element in the preview area or select the element from the Screen Element drop-down list box. Then click the Basic Colors swatch for the color you want to apply to that element. (With the keyboard, press Tab to move the highlight into the color palette, and then use the arrow keys to select a color.) For example, to change the scroll bar color from its default color of light gray to magenta, click the scroll bar in the preview area. Notice that the Screen Element text box now contains the words *Scroll Bars*. Next click the magenta swatch in the Basic Colors area on the screen. (The magenta swatch is the last box in the second row from the top.) The scroll bar in the preview area will change to magenta so that you can see how you like the new color. Continue to select screen elements and colors until you have changed all the colors you want. When you're done, choose OK.

Saving Color Scheme Changes

If you want to save a color scheme, choose the Save Scheme button in the Color dialog box (Figure 15-2). The dialog box in Figure 15-3 will appear.

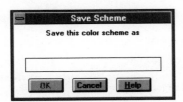

FIGURE 15-3. *The Save Scheme dialog box.*

Type a new name to save your changes as a new color scheme without affecting the original. If you type an existing color-scheme name, you will replace the existing color scheme with your modified version.

SETTING UP THE DESKTOP

In Chapter 11, "Creating Your Own Work Space," you learned how to choose a wallpaper design, a desktop pattern, and a screen saver by using the Desktop dialog box that appears when you choose the Desktop icon in Control Panel. There are additional modifications you can make to your desktop from this dialog box.

Altering a Pattern

If one of the supplied desktop patterns isn't exactly what you want, you can alter it. To edit a pattern, start Control Panel from the Main group window and double-click the Desktop icon. In the Desktop dialog box, select the pattern you want to change from the Pattern Name drop-down list box. Choose the Edit Pattern button. The Desktop-Edit Pattern dialog box appears, as shown in Figure 15-4.

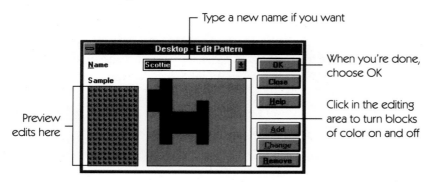

FIGURE 15-4. *The Desktop-Edit Pattern dialog box.*

The editing area in the Desktop-Edit Pattern dialog box displays pixels enlarged. A pixel is a tiny, square area on the computer screen. If you click in the editing area, you will turn color on or off in the pixel beneath your mouse pointer. Try it. In this way you can create a new desktop pattern that you can preview in the Sample area before leaving the dialog box.

You can give the new pattern a new name before choosing OK to save it. The new name will be added to the Pattern Name drop-down list box in the Desktop dialog box. Or you can save the new pattern with the original name. If you save the new pattern with the original name, the original pattern is lost.

One Line or Two? Icon Labels

In the Desktop dialog box of Control Panel, you see a boxed area toward the lower right that says *Icons*. See Figure 15-5. Inside that area is a check box labeled *Wrap Title*. With that check box turned on, Windows displays a long icon label on two lines. If you prefer the icon label to appear on one line only, you can turn off the Wrap Title check box.

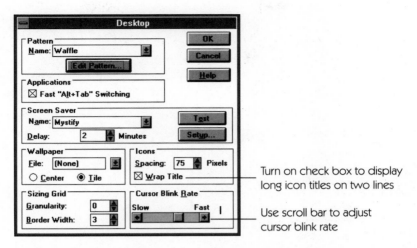

FIGURE 15-5. *The Icons and Cursor Blink Rate areas of the Desktop dialog box.*

Controlling the Cursor Blink Rate

Within many applications for Windows, you see a vertical bar that blinks on and off. This vertical bar indicates where your typing will appear and is called the insertion point or *cursor*. The rate at which the cursor blinks is an important factor in your comfort with Windows. You see the cursor blinking in windows, in dialog boxes, and in message boxes. The cursor blinks at the same rate in all the places it appears. If the preset blink rate is annoying, you can make the cursor blink faster or slower.

To adjust the cursor blink rate, open the Control Panel window and then double-click the Desktop icon. Move to the scroll bar in the area labeled *Cursor Blink Rate* in the lower right corner of the Desktop dialog box. When you scroll to the right, the cursor blinks more quickly. When you scroll to the left, it blinks more slowly. (With the keyboard, you can press the right and left arrow keys to adjust the blink rate.) The sample cursor in the Cursor Blink Rate area indicates the blink rate you select.

CONTROLLING THE MOUSE

A mouse can be a very important tool for making Windows easier to use. In the Mouse dialog box you can make several adjustments to enhance mouse performance and your comfort: You can adjust the mouse tracking speed, adjust the mouse button double-click speed, and swap the orientation of the mouse buttons. For computers with LCD screens, you can turn on a special feature to make seeing the mouse pointer easier.

To adjust the mouse settings, open the Control Panel window and double-click the Mouse icon. The Mouse dialog box appears, as shown in Figure 15-6.

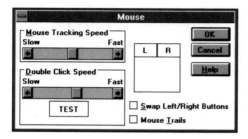

FIGURE 15-6. *The Mouse dialog box.*

Setting the Mouse Tracking Speed

The mouse tracking speed specifies how far the mouse pointer moves when you move the mouse. To change the mouse tracking speed, move the Mouse Tracking Speed scroll box. At the default setting in the middle of the range, the mouse pointer appears to move at the same speed as you move the mouse on your desk. If you have limited desk space for the mouse, you might want to increase the tracking speed. At the Fast end of the scale, the mouse pointer appears to move much more quickly than the mouse. At the Slow end, the mouse pointer appears to move much more slowly than the mouse. Slow down the mouse tracking speed if you have trouble accurately controlling the mouse pointer position.

Setting the Double-Click Speed

Double-clicking performs many special functions in Windows. A properly adjusted speed for the double-click is important for your efficiency and comfort with the mouse. The double-click speed determines how quickly you must press the mouse button a second time for Windows to interpret the two presses as a double-click. If you can't seem to double-press the button quickly enough, move the Double Click Speed scroll box toward the end labeled *Slow*. If you seem to get double-clicks when you intended only single clicks, move the scroll box toward the end labeled *Fast*. Slow and Fast refer to the speed of clicking. Use the Test box to test the double-click speed. The Test box changes color when you have successfully double-clicked it. Keep adjusting the setting until the speed feels right when you double-click Test.

Are You a Lefty? Choosing the Primary Mouse Button

The mouse is designed and set up for right hand use, with the primary (or selection) button under the right index finger. The index finger is usually more coordinated than the middle finger for selection tasks. If you use the mouse with your left hand, you might want to switch the primary and secondary buttons.

In the Mouse dialog box, turn on the Swap Left/Right Buttons check box to make the right button the primary button. For left-handers, this swap puts the primary button under the left index finger. As you see in Figure 15-7, the L|R box becomes an R|L box.

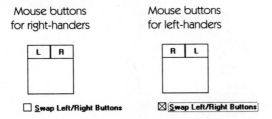

FIGURE 15-7. *The Mouse buttons before and after swapping.*

The swap takes effect as soon as you turn on or off the Swap Left/Right Buttons check box. If you turn on the check box by clicking the left button, you must use the right button to turn off the check box.

Mouse Tracks for LCD Screens

Lightweight, portable computers have liquid-crystal display (LCD) screens. Some people have trouble seeing the contrast between lighted and unlighted portions of the screen. The mouse pointer generally consists of thin lines, which can make the pointer difficult to follow as you move it across the screen. Windows provides a solution to this problem.

The Mouse Trails check box in the Mouse dialog box makes an afterimage appear as the mouse pointer moves across the screen. This overlapping multiple image of the mouse pointer makes it much easier to see and follow in LCD screens.

 Some display screens with very high resolution or with special display drivers might not allow you to use the Mouse Trails option, but for all LCD screens, the Mouse Trails option should work.

SETTING KEYBOARD RATES

You can repeat a character many times by holding down its key. The Keyboard dialog box (opened from the Control Panel window) allows you to control how long your computer waits after you start holding down a key before repeating begins. It also gives you control over how quickly a character is repeated. You use the scroll bars in the dialog box (shown in Figure 15-8) to specify these two rates.

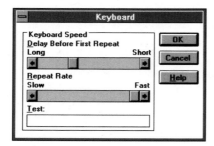

FIGURE 15-8. *The Keyboard dialog box.*

To start repeating a character very soon after you start holding down its key, move the Delay Before First Repeat scroll box toward the end labeled *Short*. To delay repeating a character, move the scroll box toward the end labeled *Long*. If you often see repeated characters during typing, you will want to set a longer delay time.

To repeat characters very quickly once repeating starts, move the Repeat Rate scroll box to the Fast end. To slow down the repeat rate, move the scroll box to the Slow end.

To test the delay time and repeat rate, move to the Test text box and hold down a key. Watch how soon repeating starts and how quickly the characters are repeated. Adjust the delay time and repeat rate if necessary.

GETTING RID OF THAT ANNOYING BEEP

Windows and applications for Windows sound a beep whenever you attempt an action that can't be done. If you find the beep annoying and want to turn it off, start the Control Panel and double-click the Sound icon. There is a check box in the Sound dialog box (Figure 15-9) called *Enable System Sounds*. You can turn off the check box to turn off the sound. (If your computer has the ability to create complex sounds, you can use this dialog box to associate certain sounds with events that occur in Windows. If your computer doesn't have that added ability, the Events and Files list boxes will be gray.)

Turn off
check box
to turn off
beeping

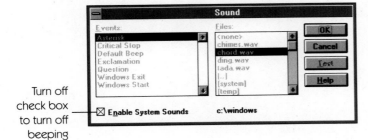

FIGURE 15-9. *The Sound dialog box.*

Chapter 16

More About
Print Manager

Print Manager enables you to continue working in the Windows operating system while a series of work files is being printed. You can use Print Manager to check the status of a printer, pause printing, and resume printing. When your printer runs out of paper or gets jammed, you can use Print Manager to start the printing process again. You can also rearrange the order of printing or remove a file from the list of those that are waiting for a printer.

When you print a work file from an application, Print Manager automatically starts. (It is minimized so that all you see is its icon.) Print Manager then takes care of sending the file to the printer. If something goes wrong during printing, Print Manager displays a message describing what happened. When the file is done printing, Print Manager closes automatically.

You can start Print Manager at any time by double-clicking its icon in the Main group window in Program Manager. The Print Manager window is shown in Figure 16-1. If Print Manager is already running when you print a work file, it will not close automatically after the file is printed.

As you can see in Figure 16-1, Print Manager lists the installed printers and the files that are being printed on each one. The line for each file contains the file's name, its size, and the time and date it was sent to Print Manager. If more than one file is waiting to be printed, Print Manager keeps them in a list, called a *print queue*, and prints them in the order they were received. The message box in the upper right corner gives you the status of the printer or file whose name is highlighted in the list below it.

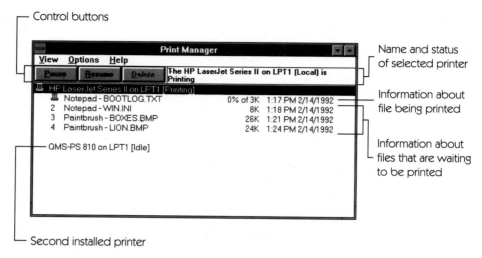

FIGURE 16-1. *The Print Manager window.*

PAUSE AND RESUME PRINTING BUTTONS

You can pause printing by selecting the printer name in the Print Manager window and choosing the Pause button. While the printer is paused, you can add paper, change the printer's ribbon or toner cartridge, or hear yourself think. To resume printing, select the name of the paused printer and choose the Resume button. The Resume button is also useful for resuming a print job after you fix a printer problem.

ADJUSTING THE PRINTING SPEED

Print Manager usually runs in the background, which means that Windows gives less computer time to printing than it does to running the foreground application (the application you are using). If you find that your application runs too slowly during printing, you can further reduce the portion of computer time Windows gives to printing. And if you don't mind that it will make your foreground application run more slowly, you can increase the portion of computer time Windows gives to printing. You can make these modifications with the Low Priority, Medium Priority, and High Priority commands on the Options menu in Print Manager. The effects of these commands on printing speed are shown in Figure 16-2.

Options Command	Effect on Printing Speed
Low Priority (Alt,O,L)	Print Manager receives less computer time; printing goes slower; foreground application runs faster.
Medium Priority (Alt,O,M)	This is the default selection; Print Manager receives normal computer time for a background application.
High Priority (Alt,O,H)	Print Manager receives more computer time; printing goes faster; foreground application runs slower.

FIGURE 16-2. *The priority adjustments for Print Manager's computer time and their effects on printing speed.*

NOTE *If you print your work on a network printer, Windows doesn't use Print Manager. A network printer is a printer that is set up so that many computers can print to it. Because most network printers have a print queue like the one Print Manager maintains to manage multiple files, there is no need to use Print Manager.*

REARRANGING THE QUEUE

By default, the order of work files in the print queue (the list of files that are waiting to be printed) is the order in which they were sent to the printer. This order is shown in the Print Manager window. The top work file in the list will be printed first. In Figure 16-1, for example, the file BOOTLOG.TXT is currently being printed, and the file LION.BMP will be printed last.

If you want a work file in the list to print before or after others in the list, drag the line containing the file's name to the new position in the list. (With the keyboard, press the up or down arrow keys to highlight the line, and then use the Ctrl+up arrow or Ctrl+down arrow keys to move the line to the new position in the list.) You cannot reposition a work file that is currently printing. Figure 16-3 shows the print queue from Figure 16-1, but with the file LION.BMP moved so that it will be the next file printed.

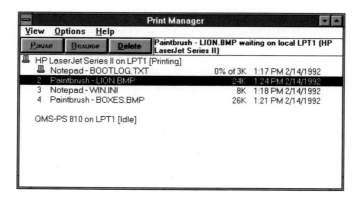

FIGURE 16-3. *The Print Manager window with a rearranged queue.*

REMOVING A FILE FROM THE PRINT QUEUE

If you no longer want to print a work file that you sent to a printer, select its name in the Print Manager window, and then choose the Delete button. This removes the file from the print queue. You cannot remove the work file that is currently printing.

Chapter 17

Networking

Many businesses are not only supplying people with computers but are connecting the computers together into networks. With networks, people are able to communicate with one another using their computers. Employees can swiftly write and send electronic-mail messages not only to each other, but to other people all over the world. Another benefit of networks is that people can easily share work files, programs, and other data. People exchange files, programs, and data by copying information to and from a network location.

Network locations, called network drives, are hard disks on computers that can be accessed by anyone who uses the network. When you connect to that network drive, you associate it with a drive letter (for example, E, F, or G) of your choice. You can then use the drive letter to access the network drive in the same way you use a drive letter to access the hard disk in your computer. Like your hard disk, network drives contain directories, subdirectories, and different types of files.

Networks also make it possible for many computers to use one printer. Having only one printer for several people makes good business sense—most people only use the printer once in a while. There's no need to buy one printer for each computer in the office.

The Windows operating system makes it easy to work with networks. If you have a network already installed when you install Windows, Windows will set itself up to work with the network, activating network commands in Control Panel, File Manager, and Print Manager. If you become attached to a network after you have installed Windows, you will need to use the Windows Setup application. See Chapter 28, "Changing Windows with the Windows Setup Application."

CONNECTING TO A NETWORK DRIVE

You use File Manager to connect your computer to a network drive. Depending on the type of network you have, the Disk menu in File Manager will have either one or two commands for working with network drives. The single command, Network Connections, enables you to connect to and disconnect from a network drive. The two commands, Connect Network Drive and Disconnect Network Drive, split the tasks of connecting and disconnecting. The steps you take to work with network drives are the same in either case, even though the dialog boxes you use look much different. This chapter describes how to work with network drives using the single Network Connections command.

To connect to a network drive, simply choose the Network Connections command from the Disk menu (Alt,D,N). You'll see the dialog box shown in Figure 17-1. This dialog box also shows you all your current network connections.

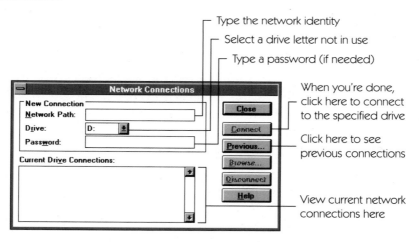

FIGURE 17-1. *Connecting to a network drive from the Network Connections dialog box.*

To make a new network connection, first type the network identity in the Network Path text box. (The names and format of the network identities will vary among different networks. Ask your network person at work for the network identities you can use.) Select a drive letter. By default, the dialog box shows you the first available drive letter. If you'd like a different letter, type it in the Drive box. Then, if a password is required for access to the network drive, type it in the Password text box. (To maintain security, the password appears as a series of asterisks.) Finally, choose the Connect button. Now you're connected!

You can choose the Previous button in the Network Connections dialog box to see a list of all the network identities of previous connections you made to network drives. The dialog box that appears (shown in Figure 17-2) enables you to select one of the previously used network identities.

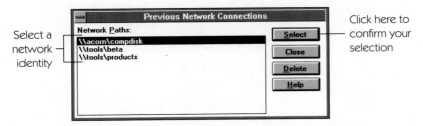

Select a network identity

Click here to confirm your selection

FIGURE 17-2. *The Previous Network Connections dialog box.*

Increasing the Number of Available Drive Letters

By default, you have only five drive letters you can use: A, B, C, D, and E. The A and B drive letters are usually used for floppy-disk drives. The C and D drive letters are usually used for local hard-disk drives (or drive partitions if your hard disk is divided). If you have only one hard-disk drive with only one partition, then the letters D and E are available for network connections. If you regularly connect to network locations, you will probably want more than two drive letters. With only two drive letters, you can only have two network drives available at the same time. If you wanted to connect to a third, you would have to disconnect one of the others first.

To increase the number of drive letters that are available, add the LASTDRIVE command to the CONFIG.SYS file that's probably in the root directory (C:\) of your computer. You can open the file with an editor like Notepad.

Type LASTDRIVE, an equal sign, and the letter of the last drive you want available. For example, to have available as many drive letters as possible, insert the line LASTDRIVE=Z in CONFIG.SYS.

After you select a network identity and choose the Select button, File Manager returns you to the Network Connections dialog box, where it inserts the network identity into the Network Path text box and moves the insertion point to the Password text box. You can type the password, if one is necessary. Then choose the Connect button to make the connection.

After you've made all the connections you want to make for now, choose the Close button. At the top of the File Manager window, next to other drive icons, you'll see a network-drive icon for each of the network drives to which you just connected. You can now use the network drive in all the same ways you use your own hard-disk drive.

DISCONNECTING FROM A NETWORK DRIVE

When you are done working with a network drive and want to disconnect, choose the Network Connections command from the Disk menu (Alt,D,N) in File Manager. As explained in Figure 17-3, you then select the drive you want to disconnect and choose the Disconnect button. The network identity will be

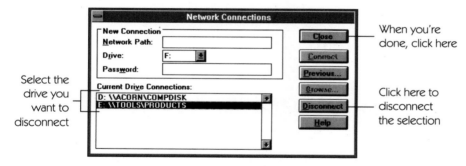

FIGURE 17-3. *Disconnecting a network drive from the Network Connections dialog box.*

Leave Your Connections Intact

If you leave your network connections intact when you quit Windows, Windows will reconnect them the next time you start Windows. This feature makes working with a network very handy because your connections are all made for you, but it means you must use a dialog box to disconnect from network drives that you don't want.

162

removed from the Current Drive Connections list. After you've disconnected all the network drives you want, choose the Close button.

CONNECTING TO A NETWORK PRINTER

Connecting to a network printer is just as simple as connecting to a network drive. In this case, you use Print Manager instead of File Manager.

Double-click the Print Manager icon in the Main group window in Program Manager, then choose the Network Connections command from the Options menu (Alt,O,C). The contents of the dialog box you see depends on the type of network you have. However, the steps you take to work with network printers is the same no matter what type of network you have. The Printers-Network Connections dialog box that appears (an example of which is shown in Figure 17-4) is very much like the dialog box you used to connect to network drives. The main difference is that instead of choosing a drive letter when you connect, you must choose a port. The ports, which are LPT1, LPT2, and LPT3, are used with network printers in the same way drive letters are used with network drives: They're the names that provide access to the network printer from your computer.

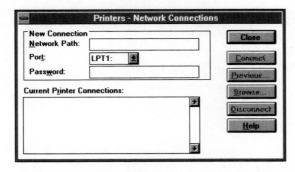

FIGURE 17-4. *The Printers-Network Connections dialog box.*

In addition to selecting a port for the printer, you must also type the printer's network identity in the Network Path text box, and its password (if it requires one) in the Password text box. (Find out the printer's network identity from the network person at work.) Then choose the Connect button. After you've connected to the printer, choose the Close button to close the Printers-Network Connections dialog box.

NOTE *Windows has the ability to reconnect network printers, just as it does network drives. If you usually print on a network printer, leave your network printer connections intact when you quit Windows. If you do, Windows will automatically reconnect to the network printers when you restart.*

DISCONNECTING FROM A NETWORK PRINTER

To disconnect from a network printer without turning off your computer, use the Disconnect button in the Printers-Network Connections dialog box instead of the Connect button. Start Print Manager and choose the Network Connections command from the Options menu (Alt,O,C). Select the network identity of the printer, and choose the Disconnect button. Then choose the Close button.

Part Three

Using the Accessories in Windows

You can automate many of your daily tasks with the accessories in the Windows operating system. Part Three begins by summarizing some common features of the accessories (and of all applications for Windows). It goes on to discuss the accessories individually.

Chapter 18

Common Elements in Applications for Windows

Part Three of this book describes the accessories in Windows. These accessories, such as Calculator, Write, and Recorder, are all applications for the Windows operating system and so have a number of behaviors in common. After all, one of the big pluses of Windows is that you can expect to control some very different applications in pretty much the same way.

So it seems right to discuss here some common elements in applications for Windows. Many of these elements were already encountered, of course, in discussions of Minesweeper, Paintbrush, and other applications in Part One. The first division of this chapter, then, is a summary of previously encountered common features; the second division of this chapter (called "Undiscovered Territory") introduces you to some new elements that are shared by applications for Windows.

COMMON ELEMENTS YOU LEARNED ABOUT IN PART ONE

In working with applications in Part One, you learned how to start applications, save your work, open existing files of your work, copy and move information within a file, print your work, and quit an application. These tasks are common to most applications for Windows and are summarized below. Most of these tasks are accomplished with commands on the File and Edit menus, examples of which are shown in Figure 18-1.

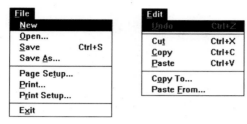

FIGURE 18-1. *The File and Edit menus in the Paintbrush application.*

Starting an Application

In Windows, you start applications in Program Manager or in File Manager, usually in one of the following ways:

■ Double-click the application's icon in its Program Manager group window, or double-click the application's program file in a File Manager directory-contents pane.

■ Use arrow keys to select the application's icon in its Program Manager group window, or use arrow keys to select the application's program file in a File Manager directory-contents pane, and then press Enter.

■ Choose the Run command from the File menu in Program Manager (Alt,F,R), next choose the Browse button to find and select the application's program file in your computer, choose OK in the Browse dialog box, and finally choose OK in the Run dialog box.

Saving Your Work

To save your work, choose the Save command from the File menu (Alt,F,S). The application saves your work using the current name of the file. (See the section of Chapter 7 called ''Saving Files and Opening Files'' for more specific information.) If you have not saved your work before, the application displays the Save As dialog box when you choose Save. In the Save As dialog box you must name your work file (following the naming conventions discussed in Chapter 7). Of course, when you want to save a new copy of a file by changing the name or the directory location, you should go ahead and choose the Save As command (Alt,F,A) rather than Save. An example of a Save As dialog box is shown in Figure 18-2.

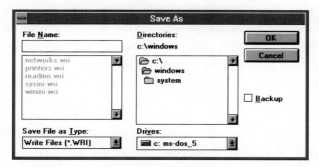

FIGURE 18-2. *The Save As dialog box in the Write application.*

Opening an Existing Work File

Some jobs are just too big to do all at once. You have to save your work as far as you've progressed and take it up again later or another day. To open an existing work file in an application for Windows, choose the Open command from the File menu (Alt,F,O). An example of an Open dialog box is shown in Figure 18-3. (See the section of Chapter 7 called ''Saving Files and Opening Files'' for more specific information about opening files.)

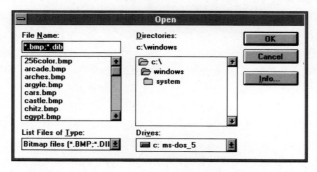

FIGURE 18-3. *The Open dialog box in the Paintbrush application.*

To open a file you must know the file's name and directory location. The easiest way to use the Open dialog box is to first make sure that the correct directory is open in the Directories list box. The Directories list box displays the current directory, the branches of the directory tree you "climbed" to get to it, and the small branches (subdirectories) that extend from it. For example, the Directories list box in Figure 18-3 shows that WINDOWS is the current directory, that you came from the root directory (C:\) to get to WINDOWS, and that WINDOWS has the subdirectory SYSTEM in it. You can tell that WINDOWS is the current directory because it is the lowest open folder in the list. To make a different directory the current one, you must first make that directory visible in the list box, if necessary, and double-click its name. (With the keyboard, you must make the directory visible, select the name, and choose OK.)

Suppose you're working with the Open dialog box in Figure 18-3. If you want to switch to a different directory found in the root directory, first make the root directory the current directory by double-clicking its name (C:\). The Directories list box will then display as closed folders all the subdirectories in the root directory to which you can switch. Double-click the name of the subdirectory that you want to switch to. Continue moving through the directories until you arrive at the directory that contains the work file you want to open.

When you open the directory you want, the File Name list box will display every file in that directory that has the application's default extension and any other common extension. (In Paintbrush, for example, the File Name list box will display all files with the default extension .BMP and the common extension .DIB.) If necessary you can list files of other types by using the List Files of Type drop-down list box. You can also list files of other types by entering a pattern in the File Name text box using wildcard characters. (For example, if you enter *.BMP in the File Name text box, Windows will generate a list of all files with the .BMP extension.) When the name of the file you want is visible in the File Name list box, you can either double-click that name to open the file, or you can select the name and choose OK.

Note that if a work file is currently open and you haven't saved changes you made to your work, some applications will ask if you want to save the changes before opening another work file. In that case, you can choose Yes to save the changes to the current work, choose No to discard the changes, or choose Cancel to continue working in the current file.

Copying and Moving Text or Graphics

To copy text or graphics, select the information to be copied using the methods specific to the application. Then choose the Copy command from the Edit menu (Alt,E,C or Ctrl+C) to place a copy of the text or graphics on the Clipboard in Windows. (The Clipboard is a storage place in the computer's memory.) Finally select the place where you want the copied information to appear, and then choose the Paste command from the Edit menu (Alt,E,P or Ctrl+V).

To move text or graphics, select the information using the methods specific to the application. Choose the Cut command from the Edit menu (Alt,E,T or Ctrl+X), which will delete the text or graphics and place a copy of the information on the Clipboard. Now move the cursor to the place where you want the deleted information to appear, and then choose the Paste command from the Edit menu (Alt,E,P or Ctrl+V).

Printing Your Work

Once you set up your printer (with the Windows Setup program or in Control Panel), you can print from an application easily. (See Chapter 12, "Printing Your Work," and Chapter 16, "More About Print Manager," for more specifics about setting up a printer and printing.) If you have set up and connected several printers, you might need to select the appropriate printer before you begin printing from an application.

To select a printer, choose the Print Setup command from the File menu (Alt,F,R). The dialog box is shown in Figure 18-4.

After you select the printer from the Specific Printer drop-down list box and choose OK, you're ready to send your file to the printer.

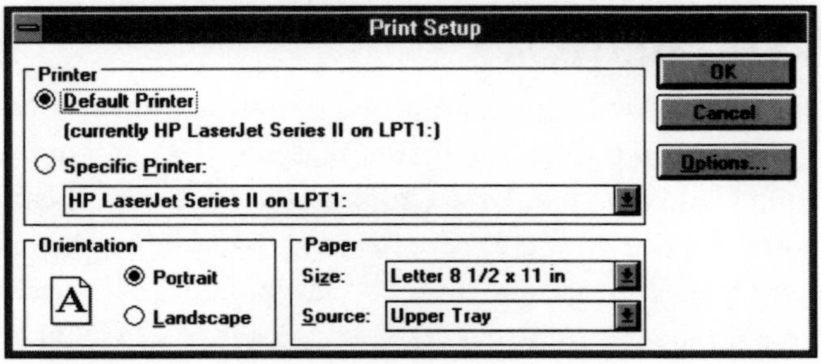

FIGURE 18-4. *The Print Setup dialog box.*

To print your work, choose the Print command from the File menu (Alt,F,P). Most applications for Windows display a Print dialog box like the one shown in Figure 18-5.

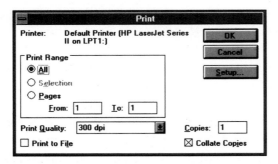

FIGURE 18-5. *The Print dialog box in the Write application.*

Change the printing options, if necessary, and then choose OK to start printing your work.

Quitting an Application

The fastest way to quit an application with the mouse is to double-click the Control-menu box in the window's upper left corner. The fastest way with the keyboard is to press the shortcut key combination Alt+F4. You can also choose the Exit command from the File menu (Alt,F,X). If you have open, changed work files, the application asks if you want to save the changes before quitting. Choose Yes to save the changes to the current work, choose No to discard the changes, or choose Cancel to continue working in the current application.

UNDISCOVERED TERRITORY

It's easy to open a new work file in applications for Windows. This process is described below. Other sections describe handy features you may not have tried yet, including the Undo command, the Clipboard Viewer, and Character Map. The Undo command allows you to reverse an action you've just taken. You can use Clipboard Viewer to see and directly manipulate the information you will copy or move. Character Map enables you to insert special characters (ones that aren't on the keyboard) into any work file.

Creating a New Work File

When you start an application in Windows, the application creates a new work file without a name. (Most applications display *Untitled* in the title bar as a temporary name.) After you save or close your current work, you might want to create another new work file. To create a new work file, choose the New command from the File menu (Alt,F,N). If the application displays a dialog box (many do not), then make appropriate choices in the dialog box to specify the type of file you want and choose OK to create the new work file. If the application doesn't display a dialog box, the application will create the new work file right away.

Note that if a work file is open and you haven't saved all the changes you made to your work in that file, some applications will ask if you want to save the changes before creating the new work file. In that case, you can choose Yes to save the changes to the current work, choose No to discard the changes, or choose Cancel to continue working on the current work file.

Reversing an Action

Sometimes you perform an action in haste. At other times you perform an action that doesn't do what you think it should. In any case, you've got the wrong stuff in your work, and you want to get it out of there, please. Many applications for Windows provide a common command for reversing actions: the Undo command on the Edit menu (Alt,E,U or Ctrl+Z).

The Undo command reverses the last action you took, if possible. Some actions cannot be reversed. For example, you can't reverse the actions of saving your work or closing a window.

Some applications indicate the action that will be reversed. For example, if you just typed some text, the Edit menu would show an Undo Typing command. After you use the Undo command to reverse an action, the Edit menu might show an Undo Undo command. Even if the Edit menu doesn't show Undo Undo, choosing the Undo command again reverses the first reversal. This means that you restore the work to the way it was before you chose the Undo command the first time.

Sharing Your Creations Between Applications

To share text or graphics within a file, you learned to cut or copy the text or graphics from the work file to the Clipboard, move the insertion point, and then paste the text or graphics back into the work file. You can use the same procedure to move information into a different work file or into any application for Windows. To copy text or graphics between applications, use the Copy command on the Edit menu in the application that contains the information and then use the Paste command in the application where you want the information to go. To move text or graphics, use the Cut command and then the Paste command.

Using the Clipboard Viewer

The Clipboard provides the vehicle for moving and copying text or graphics within a single work file and between different work files. Windows provides an application called Clipboard Viewer so that you can see what's on the Clipboard. The Clipboard Viewer icon appears in the Main group window of Program Manager. Suppose you used the Cut command to delete some text in the Write application, as shown in Figure 18-6. When you open Clipboard Viewer, you would see the deleted text, as shown in Figure 18-7.

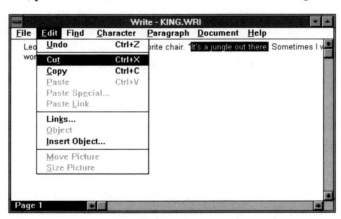

FIGURE 18-6. *Some text about to be cut in the Write application.*

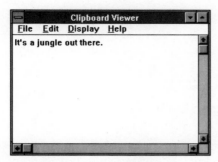

FIGURE 18-7. *The Clipboard Viewer window showing text that was cut.*

In Clipboard Viewer you can save the Clipboard contents to a file (using the Save As command), and you can open a Clipboard file (using the Open command) so that the file's contents become the Clipboard's contents. You can use Clipboard contents from a Clipboard file just as you would use any other text or graphics you cut or copy to the Clipboard.

Inserting Special Characters with Character Map

With keyboards made for the United States, it is difficult to insert special characters in languages other than English. The Character Map application in Windows gives you an easy way to see and select the special characters you want to insert that aren't on the keyboard. You'll find the Character Map icon in the Accessories group window of Program Manager. When you double-click the icon you see the Character Map window shown in Figure 18-8.

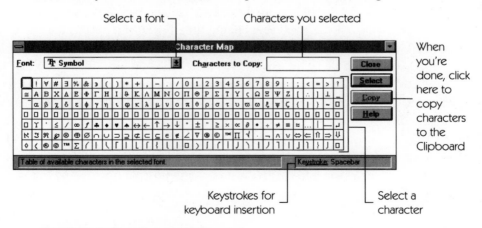

FIGURE 18-8. *The Character Map window.*

Seeing what's there

In the Character Map window, the characters are tiny. Some of the characters are hard to distinguish or recognize until you enlarge them, as shown in Figure 18-9. Character Map gives you three ways to enlarge a character so that you can see it clearly:

- Move the pointer to the character, and then press and hold down the left mouse button.

- Press the key or key combination for the character (as described below).

- Press the arrow keys to move to the character.

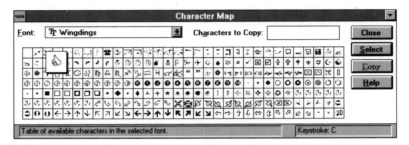

FIGURE 18-9. *An enlarged character in the Character Map window.*

Inserting that special character

To insert a special character into your work, first find the character in the Character Map window. You then select the character in one of several ways. You can double-click it, or you can move to the character (with a single click or arrow keys) and choose the Select button. Finally you can use the keystroke indicated in the lower right of the Character Map window. (See Figure 18-8.) If the keystroke instructs you to press Alt and some numbers, then you must press the Num Lock key, if necessary, to turn on number-lock mode, and hold down the Alt key while you press the numbers on your keyboard's numeric keypad.

Once you have selected the character, you still have to copy it to the Clipboard before you can paste it into a document you're working on. Choose the Copy button. Then switch to the application containing your work and choose the Paste command from that application's Edit menu (Alt,E,C or Ctrl+V).

Pasting a group of characters

Sometimes you might want to use more than one character at the same time. To build a string of characters in Character Map, you double-click or type the characters in the order you want them to appear in your work. As you double-click or press the keys for each character, that character appears in the Characters to Copy text box as shown in Figure 18-10.

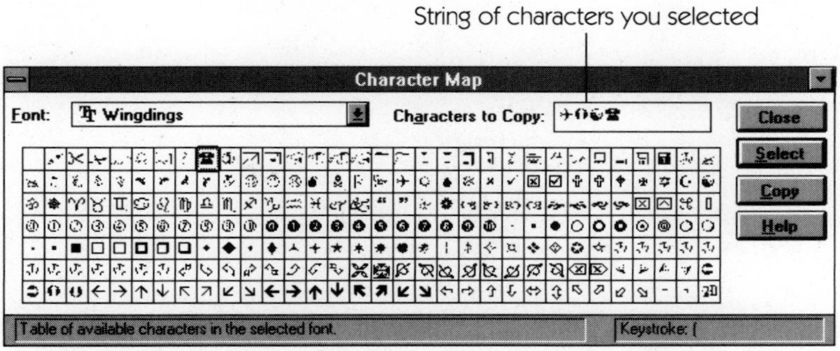

FIGURE 18-10. *A string of characters to copy to the Clipboard.*

When you've selected all the characters you want to insert into your work, choose the Copy button to copy the string of characters to the Clipboard. From there, you can paste the string of characters after first switching to the application containing your work.

Chapter 19

Jotting Down Reminders and Logs in Notepad

Notepad is a simple writing tool, without fancy formatting capabilities, that is very useful for jotting down notes and for making changes to the files that contain your computer's operational settings (files such as AUTOEXEC.BAT, WIN.INI, and CONFIG.SYS). Notepad also makes it easy to keep a date-and-time-stamped log of your activities.

The Notepad icon is found in the Accessories group window of Program Manager. When you start Notepad, you see the window shown in Figure 19-1. A blinking vertical line (the insertion point) marks the place your text will appear when you start typing.

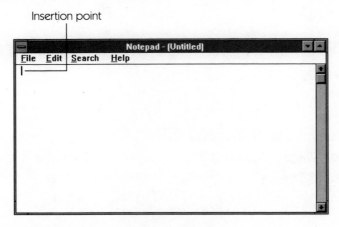

FIGURE 19-1. *The Notepad window.*

INSERTING TEXT AND APPLYING WORD WRAP

To insert text into the Notepad window, start typing. The text appears at the insertion point. You can change the location of the insertion point by moving the mouse pointer (an I-beam) to the new location and clicking. (With the keyboard, you can change the location of the insertion point by pressing the keys listed in Figure 19-7. You might find it faster to use the keyboard than the mouse—you are typing and your fingers are already on the keyboard.)

In addition to typing text, you can copy it or cut it from somewhere else and then paste it into place. It's the same basic process you used in Chapter 7, "Working in an Application," and read about in Chapter 18, "Common Elements in Applications for Windows."

Notepad starts new lines automatically only after you type 1,024 characters. Most of the text on a line that long will not be visible in the Notepad window while you're typing. As you can see in Figure 19-2, the smaller you make the Notepad window, the more you have to scroll horizontally to see your text. And when you print, new lines are started when the text reaches the right margin. Unfortunately, this means that a word close to the right margin of a printed page may be broken without hyphenation. You can solve this problem in two ways: You can press the Enter key whenever you want to start a new line in your document, or you can choose the Word Wrap command from the Edit Menu (Alt,E,W). After you've chosen the Word Wrap command, Note-

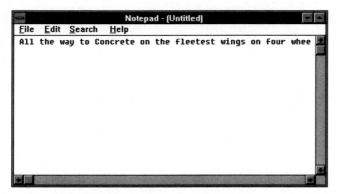

FIGURE 19-2. *The Notepad window holds 1,024 characters on one line, which is many more characters than the window can display at once.*

pad will make the text fit the width of the window, moving any words that extend past the right edge of the window to the next line down. Figure 19-3 shows the result. When you print with Word Wrap turned on, the lines of text that are printed will only be as long as the lines of text in the window.

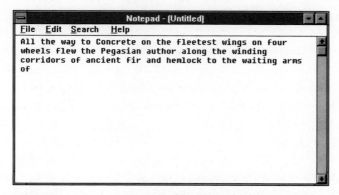

FIGURE 19-3. *The text fits the Notepad window when Word Wrap is turned on.*

ERASING AND REPLACING TEXT

To erase text, you can use the Backspace key to erase a character to the left of the insertion point, and you can use the Del key to erase a character to the right. To erase longer sections of text, it's often faster to select the section and then press the Backspace or Del key once.

To select a section of text, drag the mouse pointer from the first character to the last character you want to select. All of the selected text will be highlighted. (With the keyboard, you can select text by pressing the keys listed in Figure 19-8. Some people find it faster to use the keyboard.)

To replace text, first select it and then start typing. The first key you press removes the selected text and inserts the key's character. Notepad then inserts subsequent typing. Or you can select the text you want to replace and then choose the Paste command from the Edit menu (Alt,E,P or Ctrl+V). The selected text will be erased, and the contents of the Clipboard (the text you've most recently cut or copied) will take its place.

Inserting the Time and Date

On the Edit Menu you'll find the Time/Date command. By choosing this command (Alt,E,D or F5) you can insert the current time and date at the insertion point.

You can also set up a Notepad file so that Notepad will automatically insert the time and date every time the work file is opened. The window shown below contains a sample Notepad log file. To set up automatic time-and-date insertion, open the Notepad work file and position the insertion point at the beginning of the document (Ctrl+Home). Type .LOG in all capital letters, and then press the Enter key. Be sure to include the preceding period. The .LOG command must appear by itself on the first line of the file. Now, save the file (Alt,F,S), and reopen it (Alt,F,O). (Notice that you don't have to close the file before you reopen it.) Notepad adds the time and date at the end of the file.

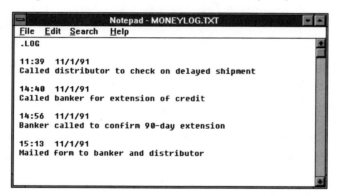

SEARCHING FOR WORDS AND PHRASES

In a long work file, locating a word or phrase can be difficult. Sometimes you're looking for certain characters because you want to change them or because they are in a section of the work you want to read. To quickly find a particular series of characters—a word or a phrase, for example—choose the Find command from the Search menu (Alt,S,F). This command will bring up the dialog box shown in Figure 19-4.

You use the four elements labeled in Figure 19-4 to specify what to search for, how to search, and when to search. The following list explains how to use each element:

1. Type what you want to find.

2. Turn on the check box if you want to search for the exact upper-case and lowercase letters you typed.

3. Choose whether you want to search from the insertion point toward the beginning of the file (Up) or from the insertion point toward the end of the file (Down).

4. Choose the Find Next button to start or continue the search.

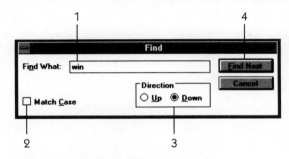

FIGURE 19-4. *The Find dialog box.*

When a match is found, Notepad highlights it. If you want to find another match, choose the Find Next button. When you locate the text you want to work on, choose the Cancel button.

To continue to search for the same text after you close the Find dialog box, choose the Find Next command (Alt,S,N or F3), also located on the Search menu. You need to choose the Find command again only when you want to search for different text or to change one of the options in the Find dialog box.

If the file contains no more matches in the direction of your search, Notepad displays a message box.

SETTING MARGINS, HEADERS, AND FOOTERS

Before you print a Notepad file, you might want to adjust the margins or add text at the top (a header) or bottom (a footer) of every page. You can choose the Page Setup command from the File menu (Alt,F,T). Figure 19-5 shows the dialog box that appears.

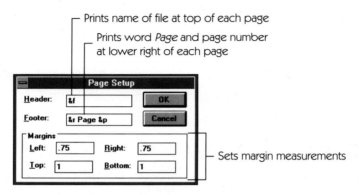

FIGURE 19-5. *The Page Setup dialog box.*

In the top two text boxes, you can type any text you want Notepad to print as a header or footer on every page. You can also type special codes that tell Notepad what special text to print as part of the header or footer, and where to align the text within the header or footer line. Figure 19-5 shows several examples. Figure 19-6 gives a complete list of codes.

Code	Prints
&f	Name of file
&p	Page numbers
&d	Current date
&t	Current time
&l	Header or footer text (which you write after the code) at the left margin
&c	Header or footer text (which you write after the code) centered
&r	Header or footer text (which you write after the code) at the right margin

FIGURE 19-6. *Special codes for Notepad headers and footers.*

You also can type the margin measurements you'd like. The margin measurements shown in Figure 19-5 give you a 7-by-9-inch print area on an 8.5-by-11-inch piece of paper.

SUMMARIES OF NOTEPAD KEYS

Many people find there are times they can work faster by keeping their fingers on the keyboard than by using the mouse. Figure 19-7 shows how to use keystrokes to move the insertion point in Notepad.

Key(s)	Moves Insertion Point
Up arrow	Up one line
Down arrow	Down one line
Right arrow	Right one character
Left arrow	Left one character
Ctrl+right arrow	Right one word
Ctrl+left arrow	Left one word
Home	To the beginning of the line
End	To the end of the line
Pg Up	Up one window
Pg Dn	Down one window
Ctrl+Home	To the beginning of the file
Ctrl+End	To the end of the file

FIGURE 19-7. *The Notepad keys for moving the insertion point.*

Figure 19-8 shows how to use keystrokes to select text in Notepad. You select text in one of two directions, either moving toward the end of the document (right or down) or toward the beginning of the document (left or up). After you select text in one direction, you can enlarge the selection by selecting more text in the same direction. To shrink the selection (for example, if you selected too much), simply select text in the opposite direction. In other words, the keystrokes for selecting text will also incrementally undo a previous selection. And you can immediately undo any selection in your work file by moving the insertion point with an arrow key.

Key Combination	Selects Text
Shift+left arrow or Shift+right arrow	One character at a time to the left or right
Shift+down arrow or Shift+up arrow	One line of text up or down
Shift+Pg Up or Shift+Pg Dn	Up or down one window
Shift+Home	To the beginning of the line
Shift+End	To the end of the line
Ctrl+Shift+left arrow	Previous word
Ctrl+Shift+right arrow	Next word
Ctrl+Shift+Home	To the beginning of the file
Ctrl+Shift+End	To the end of the file

FIGURE 19-8. *The Notepad keys for selecting text.*

Chapter 20

Adding It Up with Calculator

In Chapter 11, "Creating Your Own Work Space," you learned how to add a clock, a calendar, and a card file to your computer desktop. Many desktops also contain a calculator for quick calculations—add those bales, total the weight of that barge. Windows provides an application called Calculator to help you crunch those important numbers. The Calculator icon is located in the Accessories group window of Program Manager.

Calculator runs in one of two modes. The *standard mode* is like a typical pocket calculator. The *scientific mode* is like a specialized calculator used by scientists, engineers, and computer programmers. Figure 20-1 shows Calculator in standard mode. Figure 20-2 shows scientific mode.

FIGURE 20-1. *The Calculator window in standard mode.*

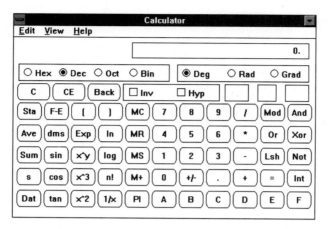

FIGURE 20-2. *The Calculator window in scientific mode.*

The first time you start Calculator, it's in standard mode. To switch to scientific mode, choose the Scientific command from the View menu (Alt,V,S). To switch back to standard mode, choose the Standard command (Alt,V,T). The next time you start Calculator, it will be in the mode you were using when you last quit the application.

In this chapter you'll learn the basics of Calculator's standard mode. These basics apply to the scientific mode as well. If you want more information about features of the scientific mode, choose the Contents command from the Help menu to learn about statistical functions, number-base functions, and other advanced functions.

CALCULATING

To calculate in standard mode, click the numbers in the Calculator window. Or press the Num Lock key, if necessary, to turn on number-lock mode and then type the numbers using the numeric keypad. (You can also use the row of number keys above the three rows of letter keys on your keyboard.) For example, to multiply 12 by 3, first click *1* and *2*, then click the * button (the symbol for multiplication), and then click *3*. For a total, click the = button or press the Enter key.

Figure 20-3 shows you some general functional areas on standard-mode Calculator. Figure 20-4 is a table of the non-numeric Calculator buttons and their keyboard equivalents, along with a description of the calculation functions they perform.

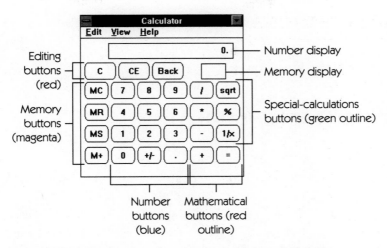

FIGURE 20-3. *The functional areas of standard-mode Calculator.*

Button	Key	Calculation Function
+	+	Adds
–	–	Subtracts
*	*	Multiplies
/	/	Divides
.	. or ,	Inserts a decimal point in the displayed number
=	= or Enter	Calculates a result (and, when chosen again, repeats the last operation)
Back	Backspace or left arrow	Deletes the rightmost digit of the displayed number
CE	Del	Clears the displayed number
C	Esc	Clears the current calculation (clear all)
%	%	Calculates percentage
+/-	F9	Changes the sign of the displayed number
sqrt	@	Calculates the square root of the displayed number
1/x	r	Calculates the reciprocal of the displayed number (1 divided by the number)

FIGURE 20-4. *The buttons and keyboard equivalents for the calculation functions of standard-mode Calculator.*

You might be wondering how to find percentages. It isn't quite intuitive. To find a certain percentage of an amount, say 30 percent of 24.99, first enter *24.99*. Then click the * button, and enter *30*. Finally, click the % button (percentage). The result, *7.497*, appears in the number display.

USING MEMORY FUNCTIONS

During calculations, you might want to set aside a result for later use. For example, suppose you are calculating the total price of an item. The total price includes sales tax. You might calculate the sales tax separately and want to set aside this number to add to other costs later. Calculator has the ability to store the sales tax figure in its memory so that you can quickly recall the number when you need it. Figure 20-5 lists the memory buttons and their keyboard equivalents for Calculator's memory functions.

Button	Keys	Memory Function
MS	Ctrl+M	Stores the displayed value in memory
MR	Ctrl+R	Recalls the value stored in memory (leaving the value in memory)
M+	Ctrl+P	Adds the displayed value to any value already in memory (To subtract a value, change its sign with the +/− button and then choose this button.)
MC	Ctrl+L	Clears any value stored in memory

FIGURE 20-5. *The buttons and keyboard equivalents for the memory functions of standard-mode Calculator.*

To practice using Calculator's memory functions, try the following calculation. (Teachers will recognize this as the way to calculate the grade for a two-part test in which the first part is worth 30 percent of the grade and the second part is worth 70 percent.) The calculation is

30 * (20 / 25) + 70 * (42 / 45)

To find the results with Calculator in standard mode, follow these steps:

1. Divide 20 by 25, and then multiply the result by 30. The resulting value is 24.

2. Choose the MS button to store 24 in memory. The letter *M* appears in the memory display to let you know that a value is stored there.

3. Choose the C button to clear the number display.

4. Calculate the second half of the expression by dividing 42 by 45 and multiplying the answer by 70. The resulting value is approximately 65.33.

5. Choose the + button and then the MR button to add the value in memory to the current value.

6. Choose the = button to see the result.

Notice that the number you stored in memory is still there. To clear memory, simply click the MC button.

USING THE CLIPBOARD WITH CALCULATOR

Calculator can supply calculated results to other applications and perform functions with values pasted from other applications. As with other applications for Windows, you share information by copying or cutting it to the Clipboard and then pasting it from the Clipboard into the work file of the second application.

To copy the value in Calculator's number display to the Clipboard, choose the Copy command from the Edit menu (Alt,E,C or Ctrl+C). Then you can paste the value into another work file by choosing the Paste command (Alt,E,P or Ctrl+V) from that file's Edit menu.

To paste a character sequence from the Clipboard into Calculator, copy or cut the characters to the Clipboard, switch to Calculator, and then choose the Paste command (Alt,E,P or Ctrl+V).

When you paste from the Clipboard, Calculator interprets each character as if that character were typed on the keyboard. However, some of Calculator's actions are specified by key sequences or function keys that can't be copied to the Clipboard. Some examples are the Ctrl+R key sequence (which recalls the value stored in memory), the Esc key (which clears the current calculation), and the F9 function key (which changes the sign of the displayed number). Because of this, Calculator interprets some combinations of characters that are pasted as key sequences or function keys. Figure 20-6 lists the characters and the actions they cause when pasted into Calculator.

Characters	Action
:c	Clears memory
:m	Stores the displayed number in memory
:p	Adds the displayed number to the number in memory
:q	Clears the current calculation (clear all)
:r	Recalls and displays the number in memory
:	Interprets the number that follows as a function key (for example, interpreting :4 as F4)

FIGURE 20-6. *The characters you can paste to cause actions in Calculator.*

Chapter 21

Keeping Up-to-Date
with Calendar

In Chapter 11, "Creating Your Own Work Space," you learned how to set up Calendar and use its alarm. In this chapter you'll learn more about Calendar: how to keep multiple calendars, how to set up time slots, how to remove appointments, and how to view the calendar in a couple of different ways.

Remember that the Calendar icon appears in the Accessories group window of Program Manager. The Calendar window is shown in Figure 21-1.

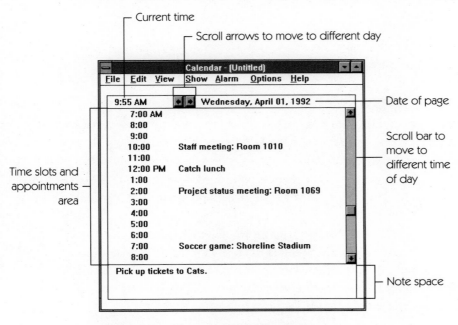

FIGURE 21-1. *The initial Calendar window.*

KEEPING MORE THAN ONE

Calendar makes it easy to keep more than one calendar. You can save appointments for a particular person, an organization, or an event in a separate Calendar work file. You just have to create another file, type the entries, and then save the calendar with a new name.

Starting a New Calendar

To start another calendar, choose the New command from the File menu (Alt,F,N). If you have modified the current calendar but have not yet saved the changes, Calendar displays a message box asking whether you want to save the changes. See Figure 21-2.

FIGURE 21-2. *The message box that asks whether you want to save changes.*

To save the changes, choose Yes. To discard the changes, choose No. To continue working with the current calendar, choose Cancel.

Opening a Different Calendar

The first time you use Calendar, you enter appointments and diary entries into an untitled calendar. When you save the first calendar, you provide a name. The name can be no longer than eight letters or numbers and must contain no spaces. Calendar will add an extension—.CAL—at the end of the name. After that, you will open that work file when you want to check your appointments and diary entries.

To open an existing calendar file, choose the Open command from the File menu (Alt,F,O). You can peruse the list of files with the .CAL extension. When you choose to open a file, if you have modified the current calendar but have not yet saved the changes, Calendar displays a message box asking whether you want to save the changes.

SETTING UP TIME SLOTS

The first time you start Calendar, its window contains hourly time slots. You can change the interval between time slots to 15 minutes or 30 minutes. You can also change the hour format from 12-hour to 24-hour format. You can set the starting time slot—the time slot that appears at the top of the calendar—to correspond to the time you arrive at work or begin your appointments. (You can still scroll the window to view an earlier time.) You can also insert (and delete) special time slots that fall at other times, such as ten minutes past the hour or five minutes before.

Changing the Day Settings

You change some basic Calendar settings by opening the Options menu and choosing the Day Settings command (Alt,O,D).

The settings shown in Figure 21-3 will produce the calendar shown in Figure 21-4, with 30-minute time slots in 24-hour format. The day begins at 10:30 A.M.

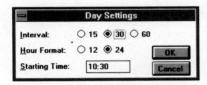

FIGURE 21-3. *The Day Settings dialog box with settings that produce the Calendar page in Figure 21-4.*

Because Calendar always displays 14 time slots, when the time-slot interval is set to 60 (one hour) the latest starting time you can have appear at the top of the calendar is 10:00 A.M. The hourly interval shows time slots through 11:00 P.M. (23:00), which is the end of the hour-format day. If you set the time-slot interval to 15 or 30 minutes, then, as in Figure 21-4, the starting time slot can be later than 10:00 A.M. For 30-minute intervals, the latest starting time is 5:00 P.M. (17:00), with the day ending at 11:30 P.M. (23:30). For 15-minute intervals, the latest starting time is 8:30 P.M. (20:30), with the day ending at 11:45 P.M. (23:45).

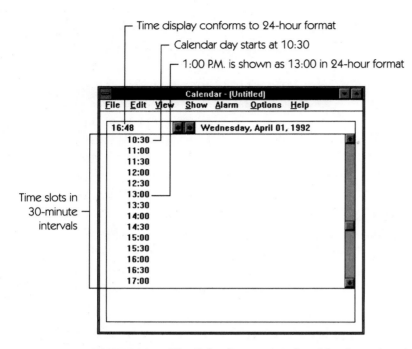

FIGURE 21-4. *The Calendar page produced by the settings in Figure 21-3.*

Adding a Special Time

Even though the three time-slot settings cover most situations, you might want to add a time slot between the regular time slots in a particular day. For example, suppose most of your appointments begin on the hour but you have one appointment that begins on the half hour. Rather than resetting the time-slot interval, you can add a special time slot for that appointment.

To add a special time slot, open the Options menu and choose the Special Time command (Alt,O,S or F7). You'll see the dialog box shown in Figure 21-5. Type the time you want to add. Then, if you are using the 12-hour format, select A.M. or P.M. Finally, choose the Insert button.

FIGURE 21-5. *The Special Time dialog box.*

If you type a time that is a normal time slot, Calendar displays a message box telling you the time isn't special. If you type a time that is already set up as a special time slot, Calendar displays a message box that tells you the requested time is already in use.

Deleting a Special Time

When you no longer need a special time slot, you can remove it. Position the insertion point on the special time slot you want to delete, and then choose the Special Time command (Alt,O,S or F7). Choose the Delete button.

If you left the insertion point on a normal time slot, the Special Time text box appears blank. You can always type the time of the special time slot you want to remove. If you try to delete a normal time slot or a special time that is not set, Calendar advises you with a message box. You can delete only existing special time slots.

REMOVING PAGES OF ENTRIES

If you decide you want to clean out all entries for a day or a number of days, you can open the Edit menu and choose the Remove command (Alt,E,R). This command brings up the dialog box shown in Figure 21-6. By default, the dialog box has the date currently being displayed in the calendar as the date in the From text box. Feel free to change it. To clean out the entries for only one day, place a date only in the From text box. To clean out the entries for a number of days, place dates in both the From and To text boxes.

To remove entries for a single date, enter the date here

FIGURE 21-6. *The Remove dialog box.*

SEEING DAYS IN DIFFERENT WAYS

Calendar gives you two ways to view days: either as a single day with time slots (as you've already seen) or as part of a monthly calendar. In each view, scrolling accomplishes something different.

Moving Through the Days

In the one-day-at-a-time view of your calendar, use the vertical scroll bar to scroll to times of day earlier or later than the times visible in the Calendar window. To change the date page, click the right scroll arrow at the top of the window to move to the next day. Click the left scroll arrow to move back a day. See Figure 21-1. (With the keyboard, use the Ctrl+Pg Dn key combination to move forward through the days and Ctrl+Pg Up to move back.)

You can also use the commands on the Show menu to move to different days. See Figure 21-7.

FIGURE 21-7. *The Show menu.*

To move to the page for any date, choose the Date command (Alt,S,D or F4). Its dialog box is depicted in Figure 21-8. Type the date in proper format (for example, *6/20/92* or *6-20-92*). Choose OK. Calendar displays the date you requested. If you type an incomplete date or a date formatted incorrectly, Calendar displays a message box that shows you the correct date format using the currently displayed date. If you type a date out of Calendar's range (before 1980 or after 2099), Calendar displays a message box to show you the range within which the date must fall.

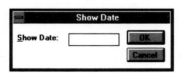

FIGURE 21-8. *The Show Date dialog box.*

Viewing Months

Calendar can also display a month of days in its window. In this case you see the days, but not the time slots. You can, however, insert a special mark in the day boxes of the monthly calendar to remind you of special days.

To view a month at a time, open the View menu and choose the Month command (Alt,V,M or F9). The calendar will change to look like Figure 21-9.

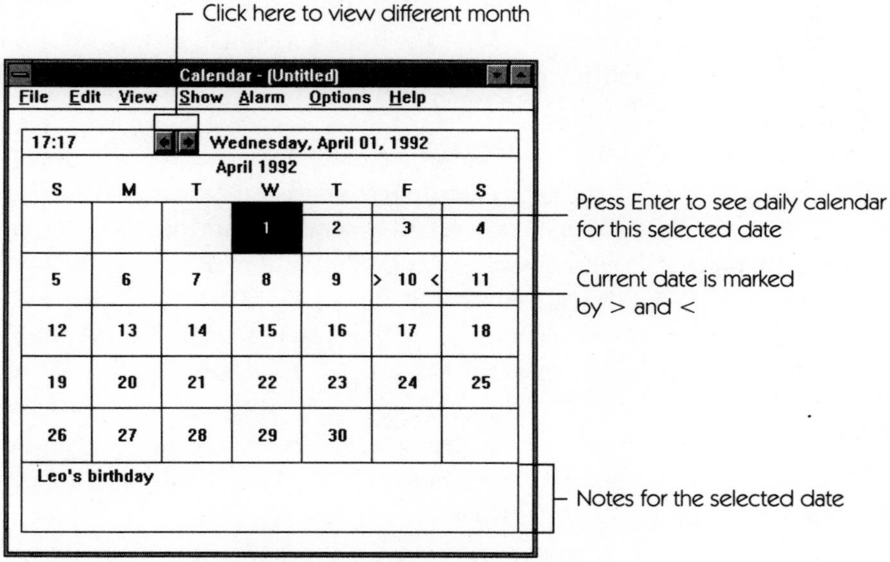

FIGURE 21-9. *The month view in Calendar.*

You can add or edit a note for a particular day in the note area while in month view or day view. In month view, the notes you add pertain only to the selected (highlighted) day. The same notes show up in both views. You can either click in the note area or press the Tab key to move the cursor from the date to the note area. Click on the date or press the Tab key again to move from the note back to the date.

To change back to day view, double-click the date, or select the date in the month calendar and press Enter. You can also open the View menu and choose the Day command (Alt,V,D or F8).

Moving Through the Months

To change the month being displayed in month view, click the right scroll arrow at the top of the window to move to the next month. Click the left scroll arrow to move back a month. With the keyboard, you can use the Pg Dn key to view the next month and the Pg Up key to view the previous one. Notice that when you change months, the same number day is highlighted in the new month as in the old month. For example, if the first of April is highlighted when you decide to change to May, the first of May will be highlighted even though it falls on a different day of the week.

Marking Days of the Month

You can add special marks to dates in the monthly calendar. Calendar offers five different marks so that you can code your date markings to correspond to different types of events. You can see the choices of marks in Figure 21-10. To mark a date, select the date either in the monthly or daily calendar, and then open the Options menu and choose the Mark command (Alt,O,M or F6).

Figure 21-10 shows the Day Markings dialog box with several marks turned on, and Figure 21-11 shows the marked calendar date (the fifteenth of April). You can see that the brackets selected in Figure 21-10 will result in a box around the calendar date in Figure 21-11. The open circle selected in Figure 21-10 results in a dot. Note that even though you can add and remove marks in either day or month view, you see the marks only in month view.

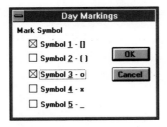

FIGURE 21-10. *The Day Markings dialog box with two settings selected.*

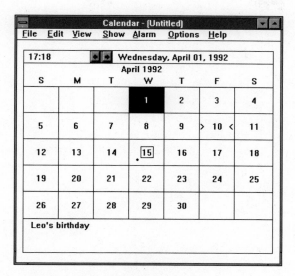

FIGURE 21-11. *A marked date.*

To remove marks from a date, select the date, choose the Mark command (Alt,O,M or F6), turn off the check boxes for the marks you want to remove, and then choose OK.

Chapter 22

Keeping Tabs on Business Contacts in Cardfile

In Chapter 11, "Creating Your Own Work Space," you set up a card file for your business contacts. In this chapter you'll learn more about how to find cards and edit them, and also how to use Cardfile to dial the telephone for you.

Remember that the Cardfile icon appears in the Accessories window of Program Manager. The Cardfile window is shown in Figure 22-1.

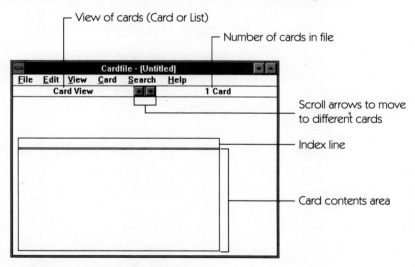

FIGURE 22-1. *The Cardfile window.*

FINDING THE CARD YOU WANT

When you start Cardfile, you see one whole card. In Chapter 11, in the section called "Collecting Business Cards," you learned how to add cards to your Cardfile by choosing the Add command from the Card menu. As you add new cards, they appear one at a time at the front of the card stack. The other cards appear as a cascade of index lines, as many index lines as can fit in the window. The index lines are arranged in an alphabetic list, as shown in Figure 22-2. If you have lots of cards, the Cardfile window can't show them all. How do you find the card you want? You can use the Go To command discussed in Chapter 11 or use one of the methods described below.

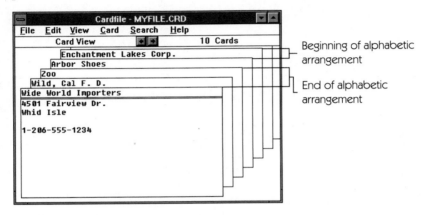

FIGURE 22-2. *The alphabetic arrangement of the card stack.*

With the Mouse

To bring a card to the front of the stack with the mouse, click anywhere in the card if you can see it, or click the scroll arrows at the top of the Cardfile window until the card you want appears at the front of the stack. (Click the right scroll arrow to move the second card in the stack to the front. And click the left scroll arrow to move the last card in the stack to the front.)

With the Keyboard

With the keyboard, use the keys listed in Figure 22-3 to move a card to the front of the stack.

Key(s)	Brings to the Front
Pg Dn	Next card in current stack arrangement
Pg Up	Previous card in current stack arrangement
Ctrl+Home	First card (alphabetically) in the file
Ctrl+End	Last card (alphabetically) in the file
Ctrl+Shift+letter	First card from the front of the current stack arrangement whose index line begins with the letter

FIGURE 22-3. *The keys for bringing cards to the front in Cardfile.*

By Listing the Index Lines

Cardfile can display a list of just the index lines, in alphabetic order. From this list, you can select an index line, and then either edit the index line or view the card to which it belongs. To view only the index lines, open the View menu and choose the List command (Alt,V,L). You'll see a list, as shown in Figure 22-4.

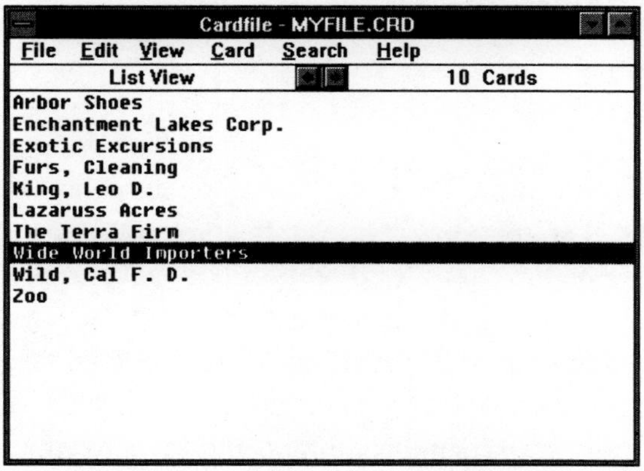

```
┌─────────────────────────────────────────────┐
│ ▣     Cardfile - MYFILE.CRD          ▽▣     │
├─────────────────────────────────────────────┤
│ File  Edit  View  Card  Search  Help        │
├─────────────────────────────────────────────┤
│      List View        ◁▶          10 Cards  │
├─────────────────────────────────────────────┤
│ Arbor Shoes                                 │
│ Enchantment Lakes Corp.                     │
│ Exotic Excursions                           │
│ Furs, Cleaning                              │
│ King, Leo D.                                │
│ Lazaruss Acres                              │
│ The Terra Firm                              │
│ Wide World Importers                        │
│ Wild, Cal F. D.                             │
│ Zoo                                         │
│                                             │
│                                             │
│                                             │
│                                             │
└─────────────────────────────────────────────┘
```

FIGURE 22-4. *The List command displays a list of index lines.*

Most of the keys from Figure 22-3 will move through a list of index lines in the same way they move through the stack of cards. One difference is that you use the up and down arrow keys to move the highlight up or down one line in the list (while you use the Pg Up and Pg Dn keys to move from card to card in the stack). To view a card when you're viewing a list of index lines, select the index line for that card, and then choose the Card command from the View menu (Alt,V,C).

If you double-click one of the index lines in the list, Cardfile displays the Index dialog box, which enables you to edit the contents of the index line. (You can also select the line in the list and then choose the Index command from the Edit menu.)

By Using the Find Command

If you want to find a card (or cards) that contains a specific piece of information in its contents area, you can use the Find command on the Search menu. To use the Find command, you must be viewing the stack of cards and not the list of index lines. The Find command (Alt,S,F) brings up the dialog box shown in Figure 22-5.

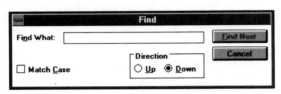

FIGURE 22-5. *The Find dialog box.*

Type what you want to find in the Find What text box and choose OK. Cardfile finds the next card that contains that text. It searches either up or down in the stack, depending on the choice of direction you make in the dialog box. Cardfile highlights the text on the card that matches the text you're searching for. If no card contains the text you're searching for, Cardfile displays a message box.

After you've found a card with the Find command and canceled the Find dialog box, you might decide later to look for more cards with the same text. To repeat the search, choose the Find Next command from the Search menu (Alt,S,N or F3). If a card contains more than one instance of the text, Cardfile finds each instance on a card before moving to the next card in the stack.

MORE WAYS TO EDIT CARDS

In Chapter 11 you learned how to type information on a card. Now you'll learn how to add graphics. You'll also find out how to undo changes to a card and how to delete a card from the stack.

Adding Graphics to a Card

Cardfile lets you paste a graphic into the text area of a card and move the graphic where you want it on the card. You need to first have your text in place because adding text later can interfere with the graphic. You also need to have an open space for the graphic because the graphic will cover any text that lies beneath it.

To add graphics to a card, copy or cut a graphic to the Clipboard from a graphics application, such as Paintbrush. In Cardfile, select the card you want to add the graphic to, go to the Edit menu and choose the Picture command (Alt,E,E), and then choose the Paste command (Alt,E,P or Ctrl+V). Figure 22-6 shows a graphic on a card.

FIGURE 22-6. *A card that contains a graphic.*

To move the graphic to the desired spot on the card, drag it with the mouse or press the arrow keys. When you have finished positioning the graphic, choose Text from the Edit menu so that you can work with text again.

To remove a graphic from a card, choose the Picture command (Alt,E,E), and then choose Cut (Alt,E,T or Ctrl+X).

You must choose the Text command (Alt,E,X) to go back to typing or editing text in a card after working with a graphic. Cardfile has two modes: one for text and one for graphics. If you switch to graphics mode (by choosing the Picture command from the Edit menu), you cannot add or edit any text to the contents area of a card. You can work only with graphics. If you start typing and nothing appears in the card, chances are that you're in graphics mode. After you choose the Text command, you'll be able to enter text again.

Editing a Paintbrush Graphic on a Card

If you add a graphic from Paintbrush to a Cardfile card and then want to modify it, you can easily edit the graphic from within Cardfile. To edit a Paintbrush graphic from Cardfile, choose the Picture command (Alt,E,E), and then either double-click the graphic or choose the Edit Paintbrush Picture Object command from the Edit menu (Alt,E,O). Windows starts Paintbrush and inserts the graphic in the Paintbrush window. Edit the graphic as you wish, and then choose the Exit and Return command from the File menu (Alt,F,X) in Paintbrush to return to Cardfile. When Paintbrush tells you that the command you chose will close the connection between Paintbrush and your cardfile, and asks whether you want to update the graphic in Cardfile, choose Yes.

Restoring a Card

If you edit the wrong card or decide that you dòn't want to keep the changes you've made to a card, you can use the Restore command from the Edit menu (Alt,E,R) to restore the card to the index line and contents it had when you first brought the card to the front. Be careful! This command reverses all changes you made to the card since you brought it to the front. If you want to reverse just the last change you made to a card's text, choose the Undo command from the Edit menu instead (Alt,E,U or Ctrl+Z).

Deleting a Card

It's a good idea to get rid of cards that you no longer need. Reducing your card-file size will save disk space and make your card file easier to navigate. To delete a card, bring it to the front and then choose the Delete command from the Card menu (Alt,C,D).

CALLING ON YOUR CONTACT

If your computer is connected to a modem that is connected to a telephone line, you can use Cardfile to dial the telephone for you. When someone answers your ring, you can pick up the telephone handset and talk.

Setting Up the Modem

Your modem is connected to your computer through a port. The standard method for setting up a port for a modem is by double-clicking the Port icon in the Control Panel window. If your modem port is not yet set up, however, you can open the Card menu and choose the Autodial command (Alt,C,T or F5), and then choose the Setup button. The Setup button expands the dialog box, as shown in Figure 22-7.

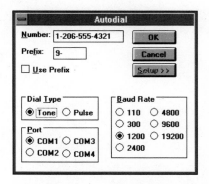

FIGURE 22-7. *The Autodial dialog box after the Setup button is chosen.*

If your modem port is set up already, the dialog box settings reflect the settings you made from the Control Panel window. When you choose OK, Cardfile records your modem settings and dials the telephone number for you. (See the next section, ''Dialing.'')

Dialing

To have Cardfile dial a telephone number for you, bring forward the card that contains the number you want to call and then choose the Autodial command (Alt,C,T or F5). Cardfile inserts the first telephone number it finds on the card (starting with the index line) in the Number text box, as shown in Figure 22-8. If you want to dial a number different from the first one on the card, select that number before choosing the Autodial command. You can also edit the number in the Number text box.

FIGURE 22-8. *The Autodial dialog box.*

For telephones that require you to dial 9 for an outside line, leave 9- in the Prefix text box, and turn on the Use Prefix check box (Alt+U). If your telephone system uses a different prefix, type that prefix in the Prefix text box. When you choose OK, Cardfile dials the phone number. When the modem opens the telephone line (the modem's equivalent to picking up the telephone handset), Cardfile displays a message telling you to pick up the phone.

Chapter 23

Building Shortcuts with Recorder

Throughout this book you've been told about *shortcut keys*. Shortcut keys are keys you can press to quickly initiate an action. For example, Ctrl+C is a shortcut key for opening the Edit menu and choosing Copy. In Windows you can add to any application's set of shortcut keys by *recording* your actions and then assigning the recording to a key or key combination. The actions that you record form a *macro*. A macro is a command that at a keystroke or two performs a task which would otherwise take you many steps to accomplish.

In this chapter you'll learn how to record and use a macro and how to delete macros you don't want or need anymore. The Recorder icon appears in the Accessories window of Program Manager. When you double-click the icon you see the window shown in Figure 23-1.

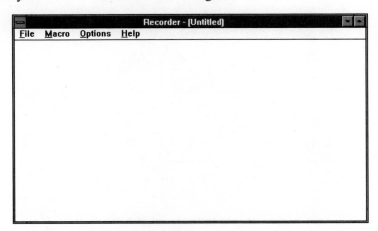

FIGURE 23-1. *The Recorder window.*

RECORDING A MACRO

Every macro you create is a record of keystrokes and mouse actions you take in Windows from the time you engage the macro recorder until you stop the recorder. (The commands that start and stop the recorder are not recorded.)

To record a macro, you open the Macro menu and choose the Record command (Alt,M,C). Figure 23-2 shows the Record Macro dialog box with many of its elements numbered. The following list tells you a little about how to use each numbered element:

1. Type a macro name (up to 39 characters).

2. Type a shortcut key (or select one from the drop-down list).

3. Turn on one or more of these check boxes to create a key combination.

4. Choose the type of mouse actions to record.

5. Choose whether the macro will apply only to the application in which you record it or to any application.

6. Choose whether the macro will run as fast as possible or at the speed you used when recording the actions.

7. Turn on this check box if you want the macro to repeat until you press Ctrl+Break.

8. Turn on this check box if you want to use other macros while recording.

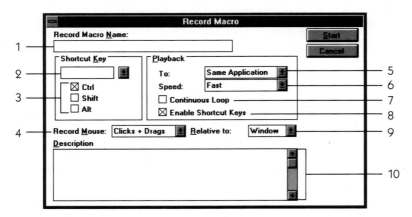

FIGURE 23-2. *The Record Macro dialog box.*

9. Choose whether the positions at which mouse actions take place are recorded relative to the current window or to the screen.

10. Type a full description of the macro.

Try the following practice to see how easy recording a macro can be. You can create a macro to minimize your application windows. For simplicity, first clear your desktop by minimizing any applications you have running except for Program Manager and Recorder. The Program Manager window and Recorder window should be restored or maximized. Then switch to Recorder and choose the Record command from the Macro menu (Alt,M,C). Fill out the dialog box as shown in Figure 23-3.

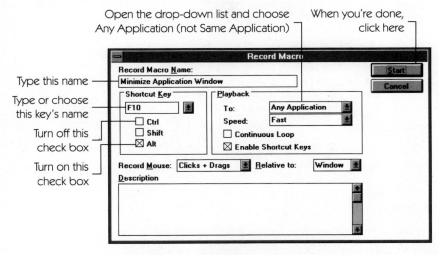

FIGURE 23-3. *The Record Macro dialog box for your macro recording practice.*

When you have finished making changes in the dialog box, choose Start. You'll see the Recorder window minimize to a blinking icon. Use the keyboard now to minimize the Program Manager window by pressing the Alt, spacebar, and N keys. (See the important Note below: Use the keyboard and not the mouse to minimize the window.) At this point, click the blinking Recorder icon or press the Ctrl+Break key combination to halt recording. You'll see a Recorder dialog box.

The Recorder dialog box will have different options selected depending on how you halted recording. The two selection possibilities are shown in Figure 23-4. Be sure that Save Macro is selected, and choose OK. You have created a macro! The Recorder icon will no longer be blinking. Double-click the icon to restore the Recorder window, and you'll see your macro listed there. Start some applications and try out your new shortcut key; you can press Alt+F10 to minimize any application.

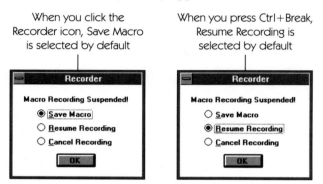

FIGURE 23-4. *The Recorder dialog box can appear with different options selected, depending on how you halted recording.*

NOTE *Avoid using the mouse when you're recording! To successfully use a macro that contains mouse actions, you must be sure that the windows and screen positions of items you point to, click, or drag are always in exactly the same spot every time you use the macro. If you are creating a demonstration using Recorder, you might be able to use the mouse successfully in a macro; in a demonstration, you are able to control the screen at all times. In your daily work, however, you might not be able to predict that a window will always be positioned or sized in the same way on the screen. Your macro could place mouse clicks and drags in the wrong places. The safe path to follow is to record keystrokes and not mouse actions—for example, by choosing your commands with the keyboard. If you do, your macros should always work as you wish.*

A FEW THINGS TO KEEP IN MIND

This section discusses a few things you should keep in mind when you're creating a macro. First, for reference purposes, try to devise a macro name that describes the action the macro performs. If you do, you'll be able to easily identify the macro you're looking for in the Recorder window. Recorder offers a Description text box for providing additional description of a macro, but you have to select the macro name, open the Macro menu, and choose the Properties command before you can see this information. (See ''Changing Macro Properties'' later in this chapter.)

The choices in the Record Macro dialog box for playing back your macro are *Same Application* (macro works only in the application in which you recorded) and *Any Application* (macro works in every application). Think about which choice is most appropriate for the macro you're creating. Choose *Same Application* when the action is specific to a single application. For example, adjusting the size of a group window is specific to Program Manager and wouldn't work properly elsewhere. Choose *Any Application* when the action you record is a standard action, such as maximizing a window.

After you record your macros, save the macros so that you can use them every time you run Windows in the future. To save the macros in a file, choose the Save command from the File menu (Alt,F,S). If your macro file is new, the Save As dialog box will appear, as shown in Figure 23-5. Give your macro file a name so that you can use the macros again. (Recorder will add the .REC extension to your name for you.)

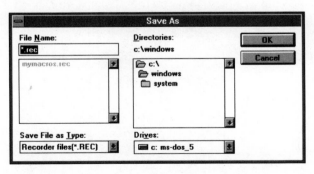

FIGURE 23-5. *The Save As dialog box in Recorder.*

USING THE MACRO

To use a Recorder macro, you must have Recorder running as well as the application in which you want to use the macro. You must also have the file opened in Recorder that contains your macro. You can open the macro file with the Open command on the File menu (Alt,F,O). With this arrangement in place, you can press the key combination to run your macro.

If you can't remember the key combination you assigned to a macro, you can also use a macro by running it in the Recorder window. First open the application window in which you want to use the macro. Then open the Recorder window. In Recorder, double-click the macro you want to use from the list. Recorder first minimizes its window and then performs the macro's actions in the application window that was active before you started Recorder. For example, to minimize the File Manager window, switch to the open File Manager window and then switch to the open Recorder window. Double-click your macro that minimizes a window. Recorder minimizes its window and then minimizes File Manager.

CHANGING MACRO PROPERTIES

For any macro you've already recorded, you can change any of the settings you chose in the Record dialog box by highlighting the macro's name in the Recorder window and choosing the Properties command from the Macro menu (Alt,M,P). Figure 23-6 shows the Macro Properties dialog box for the Minimize Application Window macro you created earlier in this chapter.

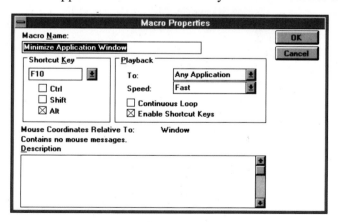

FIGURE 23-6. *The Macro Properties dialog box.*

DELETING A MACRO

If a macro doesn't work correctly or you no longer want the macro, you can get rid of it. To delete a macro, select the macro's name in the Recorder window, and then open the Macro menu and choose the Delete command (Alt,M,D). Recorder asks if you want to delete the selected macro. Choose OK to delete the macro.

Starting Recorder Automatically

In Chapter 13, "More About Program Manager," you learned how to start applications automatically when you start Windows. If you use macros often, Recorder is an application you'll certainly want to start automatically. Then you'll be able to use the shortcut keys you assigned to macros as soon as Windows is running. Also, you'll want Recorder to start by opening your file of macros rather than by opening a new, empty macro file. To automatically start Recorder and open your macro file, create an icon for the file in the StartUp window of Program Manager. The easiest way to do this is to drag the icon of your macro file from the File Manager window to the StartUp group window in Program Manager.

Chapter 24

Creating Great Works with Write

In Chapter 19 you learned to use Notepad, a simple writing application for jotting quick notes and making changes to certain files. For letters and short reports, you need a writing application that can do more with text and can include graphics. Write is an elementary word processor that comes with the Windows operating system. Write provides most of the features you need to create your documents: word wrap, search and replace, character and paragraph formatting, graphics insertion, and printing. In addition to menu and keyboard commands, Write contains *graphical controls*, icons on the screen that you can click and drag to make formatting quick and easy.

The Write icon appears in the Accessories group window of the Program Manager. The Write window is shown in Figure 24-1.

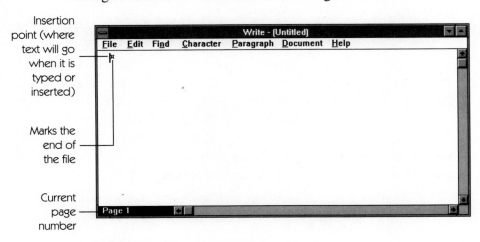

Insertion point (where text will go when it is typed or inserted)

Marks the end of the file

Current page number

FIGURE 24-1. *The Write window.*

ENTERING TEXT

When you open the Write window you see a blinking vertical line called the *insertion point*. To enter text at the insertion point, start typing. Figure 24-2 displays some text that was typed in the Write window.

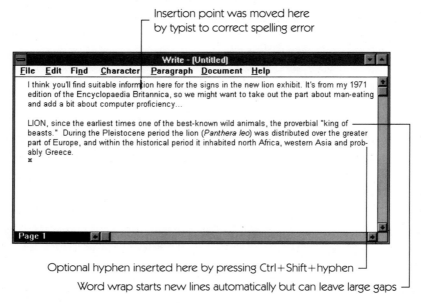

Insertion point was moved here
by typist to correct spelling error

Optional hyphen inserted here by pressing Ctrl+Shift+hyphen
Word wrap starts new lines automatically but can leave large gaps

FIGURE 24-2. *An example of text in the Write window.*

After you type some text, you might want to return to an earlier point to edit what you typed. To add or change text anywhere within the existing document, you can relocate the insertion point to that position. The easiest way to relocate the insertion point is by moving the mouse pointer to the new position and clicking. (See "Moving Around in a Document" later in this chapter.) If you have text stored on the Clipboard, you can paste it at the insertion point by choosing the Paste command from the Edit menu (Alt,E,P or Ctrl+V).

Write automatically moves the insertion point (and the word you're typing) to the beginning of the next line when it reaches the end of a line. This is called *word wrap*. Because Write's word wrap feature moves entire words to the beginning of the next line, you might see large gaps at the ends of some lines. You can, of course, hyphenate words yourself with the hyphen (-) key, and Write will wrap only the portion of the word that follows the hyphen, if appropriate. The hyphen you insert will be included in your document even if later the hyphenated word doesn't fall at the end of a line. So if you think that later editing might remove the need for the hyphen, you can insert an *optional hyphen* instead of a standard hyphen. An optional hyphen appears only if it is needed at the end of the line. Otherwise, the hyphen is invisible. Using optional hyphens saves you from having to find and delete unnecessary hyphens later. To insert an optional hyphen, press the Ctrl+Shift+hyphen key combination at the desired breaking point in a word.

MOVING AROUND IN A DOCUMENT

After you have text in a document, you will probably need to move the insertion point to different places in order to select text, to add more text, to change text, and to format text. With the mouse, you click where you want to position the insertion point. To move the insertion point to a part of the document that isn't visible, you click the scroll bars until you can see the document area to which you want to move the insertion point, and then you click at the desired location. (With the keyboard, use the keys and key combinations shown in Figures 24-3 and 24-4.)

Key(s)	Moves Insertion Point
Right arrow	Right one character
Left arrow	Left one character
Down arrow	Down one line in same column, if possible
Up arrow	Up one line in same column, if possible
Ctrl+right arrow	Right one word
Ctrl+left arrow	Left one word
Home	To beginning of line
End	To end of line
Pg Dn	Down one window
Pg Up	Up one window
Ctrl+Home	To beginning of document
Ctrl+End	To end of document

FIGURE 24-3. *The keys that move the insertion point in a Write document.*

Write also provides a special key for moving the insertion point by sentence, by paragraph, or by page break. (A *page break* is the point in a document where one printed page ends and another begins.) The 5 key on the numeric keypad, when used with the arrow keys and page keys, moves the insertion point as shown in Figure 24-4. (The numeric keypad is the group of number keys that is located on the right side of most keyboards.)

Key Combination	Moves Insertion Point To
Keypad 5+right arrow	Next sentence
Keypad 5+left arrow	Previous sentence
Keypad 5+down arrow	Beginning of next paragraph
Keypad 5+up arrow	Beginning of current paragraph
Keypad 5+Pg Dn	Next page break
Keypad 5+Pg Up	Previous page break

FIGURE 24-4. *The numeric keypad 5 key combinations that move the insertion point in a Write document.*

NOTE *To see an accurate page number at the bottom of the Write window (see Figure 24-1) or to move to a page break, you must first choose the Repaginate command from the File menu (Alt,F,E) to break the document into pages. The beginning of each page is marked with a chevron (») in the left margin. (See "Setting Page Breaks," later in this chapter.)*

ADDING A GRAPHIC

In addition to handling and printing text, Write can handle and print graphics. The graphic is first created in a graphics program such as Paintbrush and is then inserted into a Write document. After you insert the graphic, you can adjust its position horizontally, and you can also change its size.

Inserting a Graphic

To insert a graphic into a Write document, start the graphics program and then create the graphic, or open the file that contains the graphic. You'll then need to select the graphic and copy it or move it to the Clipboard.

Once the graphic is on the Clipboard, switch back to Write. The next step is to position the insertion point where you want to place the graphic, and then choose the Paste command from the Edit menu (Alt,E,P or Ctrl+V) to paste the graphic into the Write document. Figure 24-5 shows a Write document with a graphic inserted.

A graphic cannot share a line with text that was created in Write, so be sure you place the graphic in a location that doesn't interfere with your written content.

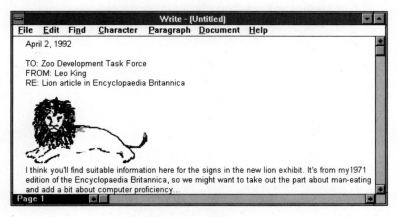

FIGURE 24-5. *A graphic inserted into a Write document.*

Positioning a Graphic

You can position a graphic horizontally in Write. To do so, select the graphic by clicking it. (To select a graphic using the keyboard, position the insertion point on one side of the graphic, and then press Shift+right arrow key or Shift+left arrow key so that the graphic is highlighted.) Choose the Move Picture command from the Edit menu (Alt,E,M). The mouse pointer changes to a box with a right angle inside it, as shown in Figure 24-6.

Without pressing the mouse button, move the mouse to drag the gray box (the *frame*) that surrounds the graphic to the new position, or use the left arrow and right arrow keys. When the frame is in position, click the mouse button or press the Enter key to set the graphic in the new location.

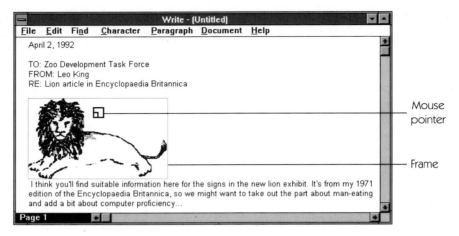

FIGURE 24-6. *The pointer and frame for the Move Picture and Size Picture actions.*

Sizing a Graphic

To change the size of a graphic, select the graphic by clicking it. (To select a graphic using the keyboard, position the insertion point on one side of the graphic, and then press Shift+right arrow key or Shift+left arrow key so that the graphic is highlighted.) Choose the Size Picture command from the Edit menu (Alt,E,S). The pointer changes to a box with a right angle inside it, as it does for the Move Picture command (see Figure 24-6).

Without pressing the mouse button, move the mouse to drag the graphic's frame to the new size. (With the keyboard, press an arrow key to move the cursor to a particular frame border and then press the arrow keys to move the border. To move two borders, press two arrow keys—one after the other—to move the pointer to the appropriate corner. Then press the relevant arrow keys to move two borders.) When the frame is the size you want, click the mouse button or press the Enter key to resize the graphic.

Notice that when you're sizing a graphic, sizing information is displayed in the lower left corner of the Write window. It lets you know how much you've changed the size. If you shrink the graphic to half its size, the display will be .5X/.5Y, which indicates that the graphic is half as wide and half as tall as it used to be. This makes it easy for you to maintain the graphic's proportions. All you have to do is be sure that the two numbers in the display are the same. If you change the proportions of a graphic, the resulting graphic will be distorted. For example, if you double the height but leave the width as it was originally (so that the display shows 1.0X/2.0Y), the graphic will be tall and skinny. If you mistakenly distort a graphic, you can always size it again to fix it.

Editing a Paintbrush Graphic

If you want to change a Paintbrush graphic in your Write document, you can quickly make the change by double-clicking in the graphic. (With the keyboard, you first select the graphic by positioning the insertion point on one side of the graphic and then pressing Shift+right arrow key or Shift+down arrow key. You then choose the Edit Paintbrush Picture Object command from the Edit menu [Alt,E,O].) Windows starts the Paintbrush application with the graphic in the Paintbrush window.

After you change the graphic in Paintbrush, you can choose the Exit & Return command from the File menu (Alt,F,X) to close the Paintbrush window and return to Write. To incorporate the changes into your Write document, choose Yes in the message box that appears.

SELECTING TEXT OR GRAPHICS

To edit or format your text or graphics, you select the text or graphics and then perform the editing or formatting action. For example, to change the word *LION* in Figure 24-7 to make it boldface type, you must first select it.

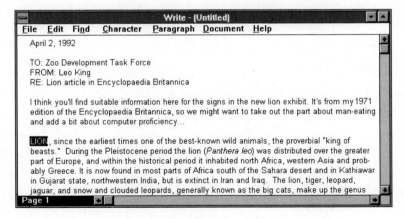

FIGURE 24-7. *The word* LION *is selected.*

Then, if you press the Ctrl+B key combination, the selected text will be made bold, as shown in Figure 24-8. Later in this chapter you'll read more about editing and formatting.

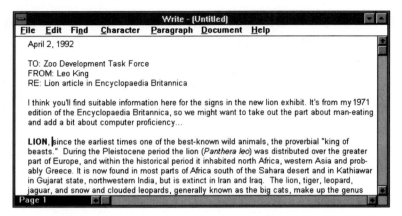

FIGURE 24-8. *The word* LION *is made bold.*

One common way to select text is to drag across it with the mouse: You press the mouse button at the beginning of the text you want to select and then move the pointer to the end of the text while holding the mouse button down. With the keyboard, one way to select is by positioning the insertion point at the beginning of the text you want to select and then moving the insertion point with the arrow keys while holding down the Shift key. Figure 24-9 summarizes the mouse actions that select text. Figure 24-10 summarizes the key combinations that select text.

Mouse Action	Selects
Click	(No selection, but positions insertion point)
Drag	Text and graphics from the point where you press the mouse button to the point where you release the mouse button. (Dragging into the top or bottom window border will scroll the window while you're selecting.)
Click while holding down the Shift key	Text and graphics from current selection or insertion point to the point where you click the mouse button

FIGURE 24-9. *The mouse actions that select text.*

(continued)

FIGURE 24-9. *continued*

Mouse Action	Selects
Double-click	Word under the mouse pointer
Click along the left edge of a line	Line
Double-click along the left edge of a paragraph	Paragraph
Click along the left edge of the screen while holding down the Ctrl key	Entire document

Key Combination	Selects
Shift+right arrow	Right one character
Shift+left arrow	Left one character
Ctrl+Shift+right arrow	Right one word
Ctrl+Shift+left arrow	Left one word
Shift+down arrow	Rest of characters on current line and characters on next line from its beginning up to the column in which the selection started
Shift+up arrow	Characters on current line from current column to the beginning of the line and characters on previous line from its end back to the column in which the selection started
Shift+Home	To beginning of current line
Shift+End	To end of current line
Shift+Pg Dn	Down one window
Shift+Pg Up	Up one window
Ctrl+Shift+Home	To beginning of document
Ctrl+Shift+End	To end of document

FIGURE 24-10. *The key combinations that select text.*

If you make a selection and then discover that you selected too much or too little text, you can modify the selection. The trick is to remember to hold down the Shift key. (If you use the keyboard, that's easy because you always use the Shift key to select or deselect text.) If you want to modify where the selection ends—either earlier in the text or later—hold down the Shift key and click the location where you want the selection to end. Note that selecting across an existing selection with either the mouse or the keyboard shrinks the selection until you reach its starting point, and then the selection begins to grow again in the previously unselected area.

BASIC EDITING COMMANDS AND KEYS

To edit text, usually you select the text and then make changes to it. If you want to delete text, you select the text and then press the Backspace key or choose the Cut command from the Edit menu (Alt,E,T or Ctrl+X). If you deleted text accidentally, you can immediately choose the Undo command from the Edit menu (Alt,E,U or Ctrl+Z) to restore the deleted text. To move text to another place, first delete it with the Cut command and then position the insertion point at the new location. Then open the Edit menu again and choose the Paste command (Alt,E,P or Ctrl+V).

To copy text, you first select it and choose the Copy command from the Edit menu (Alt,E,C or Ctrl+C). Then you position the insertion point at the new location and choose the Paste command (Alt,E,P or Ctrl+V).

The keys commonly used for editing are summarized in Figure 24-11.

Key(s)	Editing Action
Backspace	Deletes selection (if no selection, deletes one character to the left)
Delete	Deletes selection (if no selection, deletes one character to the right)
Ctrl+Z	Reverses last editing or formatting action
Ctrl+X	Deletes selection and places it on Clipboard
Ctrl+C	Copies selection to Clipboard
Ctrl+V	Inserts contents of Clipboard at insertion point

FIGURE 24-11. *The keys that edit text.*

FINDING AND REPLACING TEXT

In Write, you can open the Find menu and choose the Find command to locate a particular word or phrase. You can choose the Replace command to locate a word or phrase and also change it throughout a document.

Using the Find Command

To find a particular word or phrase, choose the Find command (Alt,N,F). Use the dialog box shown in Figure 24-12.

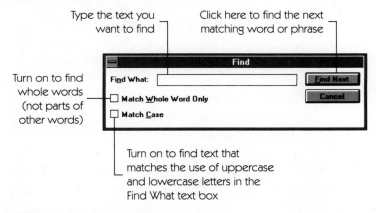

FIGURE 24-12. *The Find dialog box.*

When you fill in the Find dialog box and choose the Find Next button, the search will move from the insertion point toward the end of the document. When it reaches the end of the document, Find will continue the search from the beginning of the document and finally end at the insertion point where the search began.

As it searches, Find will highlight each instance of the text you're looking for and stop. The Find dialog box stays open, which makes it easy for you to choose the Find Next button as often as you want in order to look for additional instances of the text you're seeking. (See "Repeating the Last Search" later in this chapter.)

To close the Find dialog box, choose Cancel or press the Esc key.

Using the Replace Command

To change a word or phrase throughout a document, choose the Replace command from the Find menu (Alt,N,E). Figure 24-13 shows the Replace dialog box and indicates how to use the text boxes and check boxes.

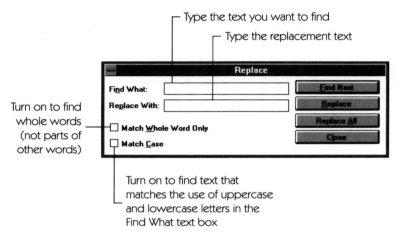

FIGURE 24-13. *The Replace dialog box.*

If you previously used the Find command, the text you typed in the Find What text box of that dialog box will appear in this dialog box by default. You can change the contents of the Find What text box, of course. Then you can choose the button for the action you wish to take. Figure 24-14 explains these button choices.

Button	Action
Find Next	Leaves any highlighted text as is, without replacing it, and searches for (and highlights) the next instance of Find What text
Replace	Changes highlighted text to Replace With text and then searches for (and highlights) the next instance of Find What text
Replace All	Replaces all matches of Find What text throughout the document without stopping

FIGURE 24-14. *The actions performed by the buttons in the Replace dialog box.*

If you have selected part of the document and you choose the Replace command, a Replace Selection button is displayed in the dialog box in place of the Replace All button. If you click the Replace Selection button, Write makes its text replacements immediately, but only within the selected section.

Special Searches

If you want to find words that share some characters, you can use the question mark (?) as a wildcard character to represent any single character. For example, if you type *to?n*, Write will find both *torn* and *town*. You can type as many question marks as you want in the Find What text box of the Find or Replace dialog box, and you can intersperse the question marks among other characters in any pattern. If you want the question mark in the Find What text box to be interpreted literally, to help you find an actual question mark in your document, you'll need to type a caret symbol before the question mark (^?) in the Find What text box.

The Find and Replace commands can find spaces, tabs, paragraph marks, and manual page breaks. (You'll learn about manual page breaks in the "Setting Page Breaks" section later in this chapter.) To find one of these items, you use a caret symbol with a specific letter in the Find What text box. The letters you type are shown in Figure 24-15.

You Type	To Find
^w	Space
^t	Tab character
^p	Paragraph mark
^d	Manual page break

FIGURE 24-15. *The characters you type in the Find What text box to find spaces, tabs, paragraph marks, and manual page breaks.*

Repeating the Last Search

After you close the Find or Replace dialog box, you can still find the next matching text by pressing the F3 key or choosing the Repeat Last Find command from the File menu (Alt,N,L).

CHARACTER FORMATTING

Character formatting is the process of adjusting the appearance of the letters, numbers, and symbols in your document. Write provides the Character menu, which contains commands for formatting characters. See Figure 24-16.

To format characters already in the document, select the characters and then choose the appropriate character formatting commands from the Character menu. To format characters as you type them, position the insertion point where you want to start typing, and then choose the appropriate character formatting commands. The text you type will be formatted accordingly.

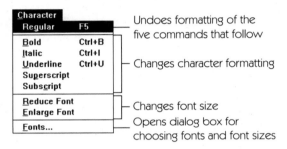

FIGURE 24-16. *The Character menu.*

The first eight commands on the Character menu enable you to change the style and size of your text without opening a dialog box. The Reduce Font and Enlarge Font commands change the size of the selected text to the next smaller or larger font size available on your printer for the selected font. (The available sizes for each font are listed in the Fonts dialog box, as shown in Figure 24-17.) The Write application beeps if you try to assign a size beyond the upper or lower size limit.

You can choose the Fonts command to change the font used for the text. Write displays the dialog box shown in Figure 24-17. The font you choose from the Font list box dictates the shape of each of the characters. For example, the default font, Arial, contains fairly square characters. The Script font, however, contains characters that are curved like letters written in cursive script. The Sample box shows how characters will appear in the font that is highlighted in the Font list.

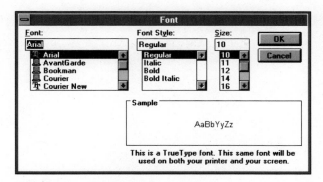

FIGURE 24-17. *The Font dialog box.*

USING THE RULER FOR PARAGRAPH FORMATTING AND TABS

Paragraph formatting consists of setting the alignment, line spacing, and indentions in your document. The settings you choose affect only the selected paragraphs. If your selection is entirely within a paragraph or if you haven't selected any text, the settings affect the paragraph that contains the selection or insertion point.

To make it easier to format paragraphs and set tabs, Write provides a graphical control called a *ruler*. You turn on the ruler by choosing the Ruler On command from the Document menu (Alt,D,R). (When the ruler is turned on, the command on the Document menu changes to Ruler Off [Alt,D,R]). The ruler, which extends across the top of the Write window, is shown in Figure 24-18.

Creating Indentions

To adjust the indent of a paragraph, drag the indent markers to the position on the ruler that corresponds to the amount you want to indent the paragraph. To move the left indent marker, you must first move the first-line indent marker (a small dot), and then move the left indent marker. See Figure 24-19. You can also choose the Indents command from the Paragraph menu (Alt,P,I) to set the indents.

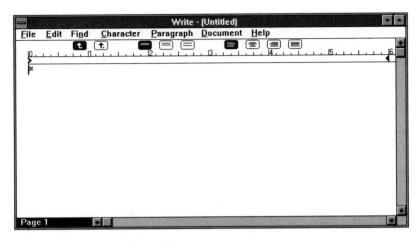

FIGURE 24-18. *The ruler in Write.*

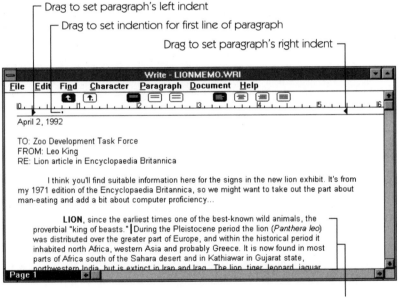

FIGURE 24-19. *The ruler indent markers.*

Setting Line Spacing

Write gives you three choices for line spacing. The line spacing can be set by clicking an icon on the ruler, as shown in Figure 24-20. It can also be set by choosing a command from the Paragraph menu.

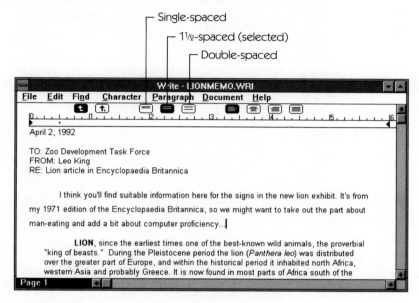

FIGURE 24-20. *The ruler settings for line spacing.*

Setting Alignment

There are four settings for text alignment within a paragraph: left-aligned, centered, right-aligned, and justified. In a paragraph of text that's left-aligned, each line of text will begin at the left margin. This is the alignment of text you're used to seeing on a typewriter. Right-aligned text aligns at the right margin. In a paragraph of text that's centered, each line of text will be evenly spaced between the margins. In a paragraph of text that's justified, each line of text will be adjusted so that it fills all the space between the margins. This is the alignment you see in most books.

Figure 24-21 shows the icons on the ruler that you can use to set text alignment. This figure also contains samples of different text alignments. (In addition to using the ruler, you can set alignment with commands from the Paragraph menu.)

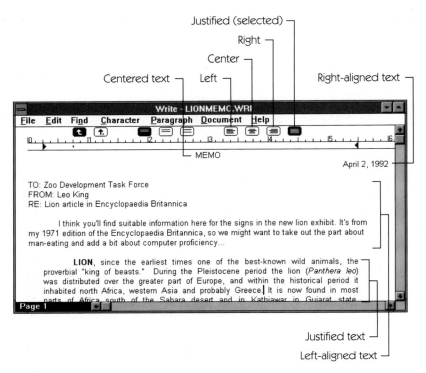

FIGURE 24-21. *The ruler settings for text alignment.*

Setting Tabs

Write sets tab stops at every half inch by default. Each time you press the Tab key, Write inserts a space extending to the next tab stop. You can also set your own tab stops. There are two types of custom tab stop: left-aligned and decimal-aligned. A left-aligned tab stop aligns text along the left edge of the tab location. A decimal-aligned tab stop aligns text at the decimal point, which makes the decimal-aligned tab stop handy for aligning a column of numbers, especially currency amounts. When you set custom tab stops, all default tab stops to the left of the custom tab stops are cleared. Custom tab stops apply to the entire document.

To set a tab stop with the ruler, click the icon for the type of tab stop you want to set, and then click the ruler at the position where you want to set the tab stop. An icon appears on the ruler at the location of the tab stop. If you'd like to change the location of a custom tab stop, drag the icon to the desired location. Figure 24-22 shows a table that uses both a left-aligned tab stop and a decimal-aligned tab stop. To clear a tab stop with the ruler, drag the tab stop icon off the ruler.

You can also set and clear custom tab stops by opening the Document menu and choosing the Tabs command (Alt,D,T).

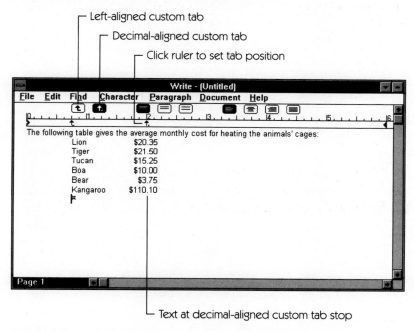

FIGURE 24-22. *The ruler settings for custom tab stops.*

PAGE FORMATTING

Write allows you to set margins and the starting page number. You can also insert custom page breaks and create headers and footers.

Setting Margins and the Starting Page Number

To set the margins and the starting page number for a document, open the Document menu and choose the Page Layout command (Alt,D,P). The Page Layout dialog box, shown in Figure 24-23, displays the default measurements for the margins. These settings are typically the ones you should use. If you do change the margins, keep in mind that most laser printers cannot print pages with margins smaller than half an inch.

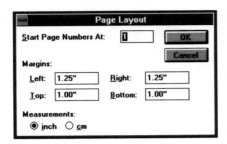

FIGURE 24-23. *The Page Layout dialog box.*

Setting Page Breaks

Write does not automatically divide a document into pages on the computer screen. To see how your document will break into printed pages, you must choose the Repaginate command from the File menu (Alt,F,E). Write will then mark your file at the beginning of each new page.

Write offers you two choices for setting page breaks when you choose the Repaginate command. You can start the page break process and let Write set all page breaks, or you can confirm all page breaks so that you can move any page break you don't like.

The Repaginate Document dialog box is shown in Figure 24-24. If you don't want to adjust the page breaks that Write sets, be sure the Confirm Page Breaks check box is turned off. Then choose the OK button.

FIGURE 24-24. *The Repaginate Document dialog box.*

If you turn on the Confirm Page Breaks check box and choose OK, Write sets the first page break, displays a chevron at the left edge of the window at the page break, highlights the first line of the new page, and displays the Repaginating Document dialog box, which is shown in Figure 24-25.

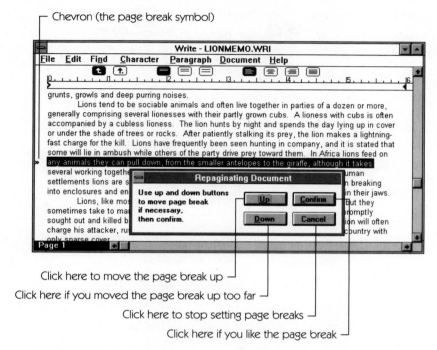

Chevron (the page break symbol)

Click here to move the page break up
Click here if you moved the page break up too far
Click here to stop setting page breaks
Click here if you like the page break

FIGURE 24-25. *The Write window and the Repaginating Document dialog box.*

You cannot move the page break farther down than Write's originally suggested line, but you can move the page break up. Write inserts a dotted line above a line of text you have chosen for the page break and places a chevron beside the line of text. For page breaks Write has chosen, you see no dotted line, only the chevron at the left edge of the window.

Instead of using the Repaginate command to set page breaks that are different from those Write sets, you can insert a manual page break by positioning the insertion point at the beginning of the line you want to appear at the top of a new page and then pressing the Ctrl+Enter key combination.

Creating Headers and Footers

A header is a line of text that Write prints at the top of every page in a document (except the first page). A footer is a line of text that Write prints at the bottom of every page in a document (except the first page). To add a header to a document, open the Document menu and choose the Header command

(Alt,D,H). Both a dialog box and a window open when you choose the header command. You type and format the header text you want in the HEADER window, and you choose additional settings in the Page Header dialog box. See Figure 24-26.

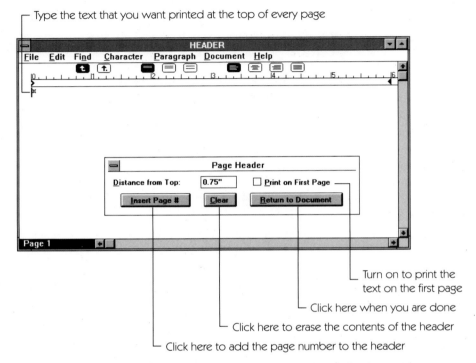

FIGURE 24-26. *The HEADER window and the Page Header dialog box, with the ruler turned on.*

For footers, choose the Footer command from the Document menu (Alt,D,F). The FOOTER window and Page Footer dialog box look nearly the same as the HEADER window and Page Header dialog box. Set up a footer in the same way you set up a header.

Chapter 25

Designing Masterpieces with Paintbrush

In Chapter 7, ''Working in an Application,'' you got acquainted with Paintbrush. You learned how to select a tool from the Toolbox. You probably played around with the tools to see what each one does. If not, it's high time.

In this chapter you'll first learn about selecting line size and what effect that has on your drawing tools. Then, you'll learn about selecting colors and the effect your color choices have. After that, you'll learn about the various tricks you can pull off in Paintbrush to do all kinds of horrible and wonderful things to your paintings. Remember that the Paintbrush icon appears in the Accessories group window of Program Manager. The Paintbrush window is shown in Figure 25-1.

CHOOSING YOUR LINE AND ERASER WIDTH

As you can see in Figure 25-1, there is a Linesize box located below the two columns of painting tools. The box contains choices for a variety of line widths. To draw a thicker line, you click a thicker line width. When you select a line width, your choice affects several of the Paintbrush tools. Most obviously, your line size choice affects the Brush, the Line, and the Curve tools. (See Figure 25-2.) As you draw lines with these tools, you see a thin line showing you length, position, and direction. When you release the mouse button, you see the finished line in the thickness you selected in the Linesize box.

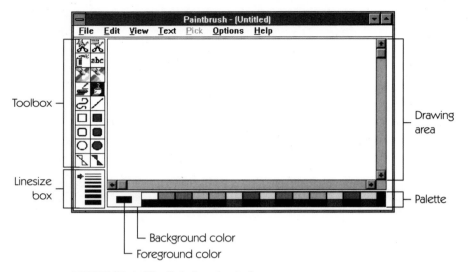

FIGURE 25-1. *The Paintbrush window.*

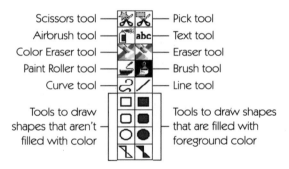

FIGURE 25-2. *The tools in the Toolbox.*

Selecting a line size also affects the erasing tools. Scribble some lines on the canvas—in fact, experiment with the various line sizes. Now, select the thinnest line size, select the Eraser tool, and drag the Eraser pointer through the lines. Select the thickest line size and erase again. Figure 25-3 shows the variation in Eraser size. With your choice of line size, you can make the area erased by the Eraser tool as wide or as fine as you need it.

Your line-size choice also affects the boundary lines that Paintbrush draws around the rectangle, circle, and many-sided shapes.

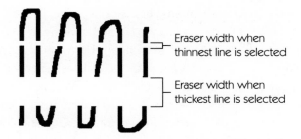

Eraser width when thinnest line is selected

Eraser width when thickest line is selected

FIGURE 25-3. *The Eraser size changes when you change line size.*

SELECTING AND CONTROLLING YOUR COLOR SCHEME

The Palette lies along the bottom edge of the Paintbrush window, as shown in Figure 25-4. Usually, the Palette shows you a selection of 28 colors for painting and lettering. You choose a foreground color by clicking it. You choose a background color by clicking it with the secondary mouse button (usually the right mouse button).

The foreground color (yellow) was chosen by clicking here

The background color (blue) was chosen by clicking here with the secondary mouse button (usually the right mouse button)

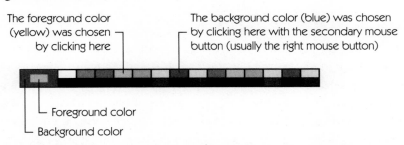

Foreground color

Background color

FIGURE 25-4. *Selecting foreground and background colors from the Palette.*

The foreground color is the color that Paintbrush displays for lines and for the border of shapes that aren't filled (the shapes created by tools in the left column of the Toolbox). The foreground color also fills shapes that are filled with a color (the shapes created by tools in the right column of the Toolbox).

The background color forms the border of shapes that are filled with color. The background color also becomes the color of the drawing area of a new painting when you open a new Paintbrush work file.

The foreground and background color choices have another nifty use. The Color Eraser tool erases only the foreground color from your painting. If your painting contains red, and you want to erase it without erasing any other colors, you can do so easily. Click the red swatch in the Palette, select the Color Eraser, and then drag the Color Eraser pointer over the portion of red you want to erase; the Color Eraser replaces the red foreground color with the current background color (so be sure your background color is set to the color you want as a replacement for red).

The Color Eraser also gives you a way to replace every bit of one color visible in the window with a different color, without affecting other colors. Suppose you want to replace every bit of red with yellow. Click red to make it the foreground color. Click yellow with the secondary mouse button to make it the background color. Now, double-click the Color Eraser tool. Paintbrush replaces every bit of red with yellow. If your painting is larger than the window, scroll another part of the painting into view and double-click the Color Eraser tool again. Repeat this process until you've changed the color in the entire painting.

ZOOMING YOUR PAINTING

As you paint, you might want to have closer control of each dot in the painting. You can zoom in to see each dot up close, as if under a magnifying glass. If you want a different view, maybe because your drawing fills the drawing area beyond the edges of the window, you can zoom out for a broader view. You can also choose to look at your drawing with nothing else on the screen. Three commands on the View menu (Figure 25-5) help you display these different views of a painting.

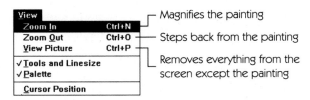

FIGURE 25-5. *The View menu in Paintbrush.*

To magnify a section of a painting, choose the Zoom In command from the View menu (Alt,V,I or Ctrl+N). If you're starting from a normal view of your painting, the pointer changes to a rectangle, as shown in Figure 25-6.

Position the rectangle that appears after you
choose the Zoom In command, then click

FIGURE 25-6. *A painting in normal view, immediately after the Zoom In
command is chosen.*

Position the rectangle over the portion of the painting you want to magnify, and then click the mouse button. The magnified portion of Figure 25-6 is
shown in Figure 25-7.

Original area that was magnified
(offering preview of changes)

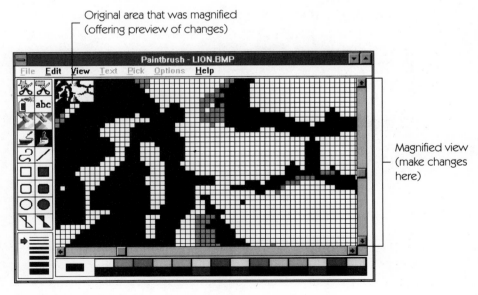

Magnified view
(make changes
here)

FIGURE 25-7. *A magnified section of the painting in Figure 25-6.*

In magnified view, you have two tools available: Brush and Paint Roller. To change the color of a little square (called a *pixel*) in your drawing, choose the Brush tool and select the foreground color you want the pixel to have. Click the pixel to make the change. To ''erase'' a pixel, click the secondary mouse button (usually the right one) and the pixel will be replaced with the current background color. To work beyond the edge of what you see in the window, use the scroll bars to move to other parts of the painting.

Use the Paint Roller tool only if you want to change the color of an area. (The Paint Roller tool fills an outlined area with the foreground color.) Note that the color from Paint Roller flows only as far as the edge of the window. You may need to scroll the window to change the color of a larger area.

You can choose the Zoom Out command from the View menu (Alt,V,O or Ctrl+O) to return the picture to a normal view from a magnified view.

Then, when you have a normal view of your painting, you can choose the Zoom Out command to give you a view of the entire drawing area, as shown in Figure 25-8. In the expanded view, only the Pick tool is available. You can select and copy or cut a portion of the painting. Use this expanded view to copy or cut a painting that is larger than the window when Paintbrush is in normal view (but see the Tip below about ''Pasting a Picture That Is Larger than the Normal View Window'').

FIGURE 25-8. *The whole drawing area of the painting from Figure 25-6.*

Pasting a Picture That Is Larger than the Normal View Window

If your Paintbrush window is in normal view and you want to paste a picture from the Clipboard that is larger than the normal view, you need to first use the Zoom Out command (Alt,V,O or Ctrl+O) to expand the view to the entire drawing area. If you don't use the Zoom Out command first, the large picture that you try to paste will be cut off at the edges of the drawing area. Only the section of the picture that fits inside the normal view window will be pasted.

When you paste a picture into the expanded view, you will see cross-hatching in place of the picture, as shown below. The Paste process is not complete while the cross-hatching is visible. If you switch to normal view when the cross-hatching is displayed, the picture you pasted will not be retained in your drawing.

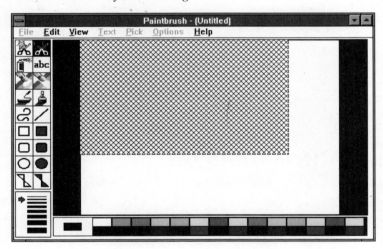

After you paste a picture in expanded view, click anywhere outside the cross-hatching in the drawing area, or click the Toolbox. The pasted picture will then be displayed, and the cross-hatching will be gone.

To return to normal view from the view of the whole drawing area, choose the Zoom In command (Alt,V,I or Ctrl+N). In this case, the pointer does not change to a rectangle.

To see just your painting on the screen, with nothing else on the screen, choose the View Picture command (Alt,V,V or Ctrl+P). See Figure 25-9.

To return to the Paintbrush window from the picture view, click the mouse button or press any key.

FIGURE 25-9. *A view of the painting with nothing else on the screen.*

WORKING WITH CUTOUTS

In Chapter 7, "Working in an Application," you learned how to select a part of a Paintbrush picture. This selection is called a *cutout,* and Paintbrush gives you a number of options for manipulating cutouts. In the sections that follow you'll learn, among other things, how to move, copy, smear, shrink, enlarge, tilt, flip, and invert a cutout.

Moving a Cutout

To move part of a painting, select the part you want to move with the Scissors or the Pick tool, move the mouse pointer inside the dotted outline so that the cross hair changes to an arrow, drag the selected part to its new position, and then release the mouse button.

If the cutout you are moving is not completely filled in with a foreground color, you can move the cutout as a transparent cutout or as an opaque cutout. A transparent cutout allows you to ''see through'' the background color in the cutout to the drawing beneath it. An opaque cutout hides any drawing that is beneath it. For example, suppose you're working with the drawing shown in Figure 25-10.

FIGURE 25-10. *A circle and a square drawn in Paintbrush.*

If you select the circle and move the cutout over the square as a transparent cutout, as shown in Figure 25-11, the square will be visible through the ''empty'' parts of the cutout.

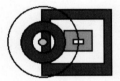

FIGURE 25-11. *The transparent cutout over the square.*

The ''empty'' parts of the cutout are the parts that are in the background color. In the example, the background color is white, so pieces of the square are visible in the white portions of the circle.

If, however, you move the cutout over the square as an opaque cutout, the square will be hidden by the cutout, as shown in Figure 25-12.

FIGURE 25-12. *The opaque cutout over the square.*

To move the cutout as a transparent cutout, you drag it in the usual way. To move the cutout as an opaque cutout, you drag it by using the secondary mouse button. (The secondary mouse button is usually the right button.)

Copying a Cutout

You can also drag a selected area to copy a cutout while leaving the original picture intact. You just have to hold down the Ctrl key while you drag. Here's what you do: Select an area and move the mouse pointer inside the dotted outline so that the pointer's shape changes from a cross hair to an arrow. Then hold down the Ctrl key while you drag a copy of the selected part to its new position, and release the Ctrl key and the mouse button.

If the selection you are copying is not completely filled in with a foreground color, you can create a transparent cutout (meaning you can "see through" the background color in the cutout) or as an opaque cutout (meaning you can't "see through" it). See Figure 25-11 for an example of a transparent cutout and Figure 25-12 for an example of an opaque cutout. To copy a transparent cutout, use the primary mouse button (usually the left one) with the Ctrl key to drag a copy of the cutout. To copy an opaque cutout, use the secondary mouse button (usually the right one) with the Ctrl key to drag a copy of the cutout.

Smearing a Cutout

Smearing a cutout makes many copies that overlap each other, either as transparent cutouts or as opaque cutouts. As you can see in Figure 25-13, transparent smears can create striking effects.

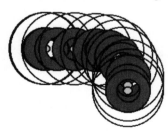

FIGURE 25-13. *A transparent smear.*

To smear a cutout, select an area with the Scissors or Pick tool and move the mouse pointer inside the dotted outline so that the pointer's shape changes from a cross hair to an arrow. Then hold down the Shift key while you drag the selected part across the drawing area, and release the Shift key and the mouse button. A transparent smear is created by dragging normally, while an opaque smear is created by dragging with the secondary mouse button pressed. (The secondary mouse button is usually the right mouse button.)

Shrinking or Enlarging a Cutout

After you create a painting, you might want it smaller or larger than the size you painted it. Or, you might want to make copies of a shape you created, with some copies smaller and others larger than the original shape's size. Paintbrush provides the Shrink + Grow command on the Pick menu to make a smaller or larger copy of a painting as shown in Figure 25-14.

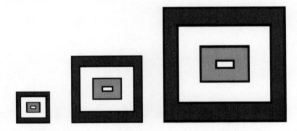

FIGURE 25-14. *A graphic with smaller copy (left) and larger copy (right).*

To make a smaller or larger copy of a cutout, select the area to be copied with the Scissors tool or Pick tool, and choose the Shrink + Grow command from the Pick menu (Alt,P,S). Then drag the pointer in the drawing area to form a rectangle of the size and shape you want the copy to be, and release the mouse button. To make the copy the same proportions as the original selection, hold down the Shift key as you drag the mouse pointer.

The Shrink + Grow command remains turned on until you turn it off by choosing the command again. This feature makes it possible to copy the original many times in various sizes. If you want to remove the original when you create the larger or smaller copy, open the Pick menu and choose the Clear command (Alt,P,C) before making the copy. Turn off the Clear command again when you want to keep the original as well as the copies.

Tilting a Cutout

If you'd like to create a tilted copy of a cutout, open the Pick menu and choose the Tilt command to make either a right-leaning or a left-leaning copy of a graphic. Figure 25-15 gives examples.

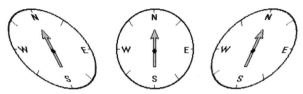

FIGURE 25-15. *A graphic with copies that have left-leaning and right-leaning tilts.*

To make a tilted copy of a cutout, select an area with the Scissors tool or Pick tool, and choose the Tilt command from the Pick menu (Alt,P,T). Then drag the pointer left or right in the area of the drawing where you want the tilted copy to be. You will see a rectangle the size of the cutout tilting as you drag the pointer. Release the mouse button when the tilt is the way you'd like.

The Tilt command remains turned on until you turn it off by choosing the command again. This feature makes it possible to make many tilted copies of the cutout at various angles. If you want to remove the original drawing when you create a tilted copy, choose the Clear command (Alt,P,C) before making the copy. Turn off the Clear command again when you want to keep the original as well as the copies.

If you want the tilted copy to be a different size from the original, first make a copy in the new size with the Shrink + Grow command. Turn off the Shrink + Grow command, select the new copy, and then choose the Tilt command to draw the tilted cutout.

Flipping a Cutout

After you paint an object, you might want to use it in a different orientation. Being able to change the orientation of a cutout can be useful when you want to paint half of an object and then copy it to use as the other half. But to do so, you need to flip the copy over so it "faces" the opposite direction. You can flip a cutout both horizontally and vertically. You can also apply both horizontal and vertical flips to the same graphic. Figure 25-16 shows the four possible orientations.

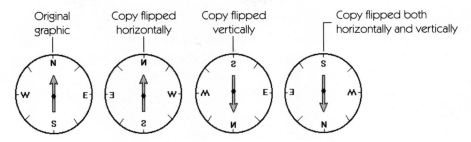

FIGURE 25-16. *The four orientations of a cutout.*

To flip a cutout, select the cutout with the Scissors or Pick tool. To flip the cutout horizontally, choose Flip Horizontal from the Pick menu (Alt,P,H). To flip the cutout vertically, choose Flip Vertical (Alt,P,V). You can flip the cutout in both directions as many times as you want.

Inverting a Cutout

Sometimes a painting might look better, or at least different, if the colors were inverted. By choosing the Inverse command from the Pick menu (Alt,P,I), you turn black to white, white to black, and other colors to their opposites. You can see an example in Figure 25-17.

FIGURE 25-17. *A drawing and an inverted copy.*

PRINTING YOUR PAINTING

Printing in Paintbrush is similar to printing in other Windows applications. You choose the Print command from the File menu (Alt,F,P). Figure 25-18 shows this dialog box with the elements numbered, and the following list tells you a little about how to use each numbered element:

1. Choose this option to print a lower quality picture at top printer speed.

2. Choose this option to print the highest quality picture.

3. Choose this option to print the entire drawing.

4. Choose this option to print part of the drawing. (In order to print part of a drawing, you have to choose this option, make other choices in the dialog box, and finally choose OK. Then you must select a cutout in your drawing. When you release the mouse button after making the selection, printing of the selection will start.)

5. Type the number of copies to print.

6. Turn on this check box to print at the printer's resolution rather than the screen's. (Different printers print pixels in different sizes. If this check box is turned on, the size of the pixels—and the size of the drawing—depends on the printer you are using. If the check box is turned off, Paintbrush makes sure that the size of the printed drawing matches the size of the drawing on the screen.)

7. Type a percentage that indicates the relative size of the printed image compared to the original graphic. (In other words, 100% means that the printed image and the graphic on the screen are of corresponding size. A percentage under 100% means that the printed image is smaller than the graphic; a percentage over 100% means that the printer image is larger.)

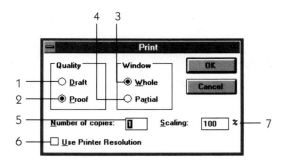

FIGURE 25-18. *The Print dialog box.*

Chapter 26

Connecting with Terminal

The Terminal application provided with the Windows operating system enables you to connect to any computer over telephone lines. While you're connected, Terminal enables you to type messages and receive responses. You can also send files to the other computer or receive files from it. With Terminal you can connect to *online information services* such as CompuServe and GEnie. These online services give you information on just about any topic and let you read and write messages on *electronic bulletin boards*.

To use Terminal, you'll need a *modem* that is attached to your computer and to a phone line. (A modem is a device that makes it possible to transmit and receive information over the phone line. Because your computer and the phone lines work with information in different formats, you need to use a modem to translate the information to the proper format.) With the modem in place, the Terminal application performs two functions. First, it dials the phone number and connects to another computer for you, using settings that you specify. Second, it acts as your link to the other computer. After you connect, everything you see in the Terminal window (except what you type) comes from the other computer via the phone line. When you type something in the Terminal window, the information you type is sent—again via the phone line—to be handled by the other computer.

The Terminal icon appears in the Accessories group window of Program Manager. The first time you double-click the icon, you see the Terminal window and a dialog box, as shown in Figure 26-1.

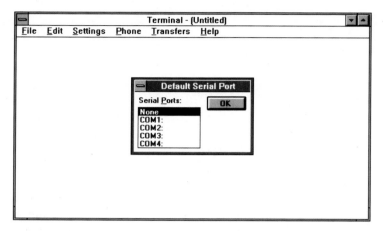

FIGURE 26-1. *The Terminal window the first time you start Terminal.*

Select the port to which your modem is connected, and choose the OK button. (Ports are described later in this chapter.) If you're unsure about what port to select, select *None*. The following section tells you how to change your selection later.

SETTING UP

When you talk to someone you don't know, the first thing you do is find out whether you speak the same language. Similarly, the first time you connect your computer to another computer, you must be sure that the two computers "speak the same language." To do this, you set up a communications file. This file contains the settings that let Terminal know exactly how to connect to the other computer. The next time you connect to that computer, you can use the communications file that you set up the first time.

You use the commands on the Settings menu to set up the communications file. This menu is shown in Figure 26-2.

You must choose some of these commands before you can conduct a communications session with another computer. At the very least, you need to provide a telephone number for Terminal to dial (the Phone Number command), you need to specify the port to which your modem is connected (the Communications command), and you need to specify the type of modem you have (the Modem Commands command). The default settings provided by the

FIGURE 26-2. *The Settings menu.*

other commands are correct for most cases. If you have trouble connecting with the other computer, adjust the settings provided by the Communications command. If you are connected to an online service, such as CompuServe or GEnie, check the books the service provided when you signed up, to be sure you have the correct settings. If you are connecting to a computer at a business, check with the computer operator there for the proper settings. If you continue to have trouble after you connect (for example, if the characters that appear in the window are unreadable), try adjusting the settings provided by the Terminal Emulation and Terminal Preferences commands. (All of these commands are discussed in more detail below.)

When you're done setting up, choose the Save command from the File menu (Alt,F,S) to save the settings in a communications file. The communications file will have a name with at most eight letters (no spaces) and the extension .TRM. The next time you want to communicate with the same computer, all you have to do to set up is open that communications file by choosing the Open command from the File menu (Alt,F,O).

Setting the Phone Number

To connect to another computer, you need to have Terminal dial its telephone number. First, however, you need to tell Terminal the number to dial.

To provide Terminal with the telephone number of the other computer, choose the Phone Number command from the Settings menu (Alt,S,N). Terminal displays the dialog box shown in Figure 26-3. You type the telephone number in the Dial text box. Include the area code for long distance. If you need to first dial a number to get an outside line (usually a 9), type the number followed by a comma.

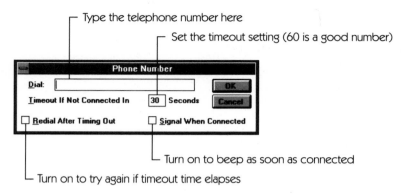

FIGURE 26-3. *The Phone Number dialog box.*

If you turn on the Redial After Timing Out check box in the Phone Number dialog box, Terminal will keep trying to connect to the other computer. If you turn off the Redial After Timing Out check box and Terminal makes no connection the first time it tries, Terminal hangs up.

Communications Settings

Before Terminal can use the modem to dial the number, it has to know to which communications port the modem is connected. You plug a cable from your modem into a communications port at the back of your computer. Most often you have two ports to choose from. They're called COM1 and COM2, which stand for communications ports 1 and 2.

There is no need to specify a port during the setup process if you specified the correct communications port the first time you started Terminal. However, if you didn't specify a communications port or if you changed the port, choose the Communications command from the Settings menu (Alt,S,C) and select the appropriate port name from the Connector list box.

You also use the Communications dialog box (Figure 26-4) to set the communications speed that the modem will use. It's important that both modems (yours and the one attached to the other computer) are working at the same speed. The most common speeds these days are 1200 baud and 2400 baud. (Baud is a measure of the amount of information that can be sent per second.)

The other settings in the Communications dialog box should be correct. If you have trouble with communications, consult the documentation for the online service or consult the operator of the other computer.

Choose the speed of communications

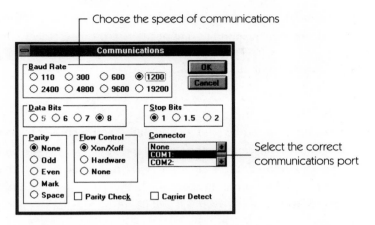

Select the correct communications port

FIGURE 26-4. *The Communications dialog box.*

Modem Commands

Each type of modem accepts special codes for its various commands. The codes are usually a series of letters, numbers, and symbols. To provide Terminal with the correct codes for your type of modem, choose the Modem Commands command from the Settings menu (Alt,S,D). As you can see in Figure 26-5, the Modem Commands dialog box includes an area labeled *Modem Defaults*. Select your modem type from the list. The correct codes will appear in the area of the dialog box labeled *Commands*. (Because many modems use the commands that were developed originally for the Hayes modem, the Hayes defaults are preset.)

Special codes for the Hayes modem are entered in this area

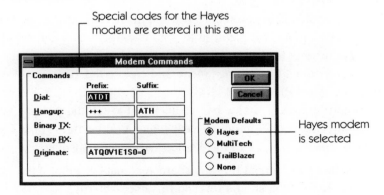

Hayes modem is selected

FIGURE 26-5. *The Modem Commands dialog box.*

259

If you don't know the type of modem you own, check your modem manual. If its type doesn't correspond to one of the listed types, select None in the Modem Defaults area and fill in the Commands text boxes yourself. Your modem manual will tell you what codes to enter.

Terminal Emulation

While your computer is connected to another computer, your computer acts as a terminal, which means it functions as the screen and keyboard for the other computer. Terminal can emulate three popular types of computer terminal. To set which type Terminal should emulate, choose the Terminal Emulation command from the Settings menu (Alt,S,T). The resulting dialog box is shown in Figure 26-6.

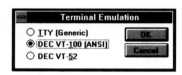

FIGURE 26-6. *The Terminal Emulation dialog box.*

Check your online service documentation or check with the operator of the other computer for the proper terminal emulation type. If you are unsure, select DEC VT-100 (ANSI). If you have problems with that emulation, select TTY (Generic).

Terminal Preferences

With the Terminal Preferences command, you can make the text in your Terminal window more legible and pleasing to your eye. Also, you can set options for how your terminal behaves during a communications session. To set terminal preferences, open the Settings menu and choose the Terminal Preferences command (Alt,S,P).

The Terminal Preferences dialog box enables you to set many characteristics of the display. Figure 26-7 numbers each element of the dialog box. The following list describes how each of the elements affects the display.

1. Turn on to move to the next line any characters that extend past the specified column. You should turn on this check box if the other computer displays 132 columns but you display 80.

2. Turn on to have your computer display the characters you type. Usually the other computer displays the characters you type for you, so you won't have to turn on this check box.

3. Turn on to hear beeps from the other computer.

4. Choose the number of columns displayed on your screen. Usually the number is 80.

5. Select a font and a font size.

6. Turn on to make it possible to scroll the window to see earlier parts of the communications session.

7. Turn on to have Windows use the function keys, arrow keys, and key combinations that include the Ctrl key. Turn off to send these keys and key combinations to the other computer.

8. Turn on if lines of characters sent to you by the other computer overlap. Turn off if the text is double-spaced.

9. Turn on if lines of characters you type overlap. Turn off if the text is double-spaced.

10. Select the cursor form.

11. Turn on for a blinking cursor. Turn off for a solid cursor.

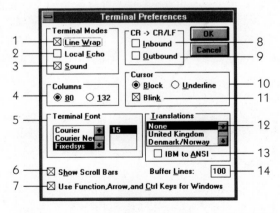

FIGURE 26-7. *The Terminal Preferences dialog box.*

12. If connecting to a foreign computer, select the language. Because different languages use different characters (some require accented letters, for example), the language you choose determines the characters that will be sent.

13. Turn on if using a language that includes extended characters such as Æ or accented characters.

14. Type the number of lines of the communications session that will be kept in computer memory. You can save from 25 to 399 lines. Terminal will keep only the number of lines you specify in its window. If you specify 100 lines, you can use the scroll bar to see the last 100 lines of your communications session. If you want access to most of your session, specify 399.

MAKING CONNECTION

With the phone number and other settings in place, you're now ready to make a connection to another computer. You can either use the file that's currently open or choose another communications file (that has the extension .TRM) with a different phone number and other settings. To open a new communications file, choose the Open command from the File menu (Alt,F,O).

With your communications file open, you connect to the other computer by opening the Phone menu and choosing the Dial command (Alt,P,D). As shown in Figure 26-8, Terminal displays the number being dialed and the amount of time left before the attempt to connect fails. You will also see some modem commands in the Terminal window. These are the commands that the modem uses to open the phone line and dial the number. You set these commands in the Modem Commands dialog box.

In order for your computer to connect successfully to another computer, the other computer's modem must answer the phone by sending a sound that is unique to modems. When your modem receives the sound, it knows that it has reached the other computer. You can then begin transferring information. If you get a busy signal or if the other computer isn't set up to answer the phone, the attempt to connect will fail. You can cancel the connection at any time by choosing the Cancel button.

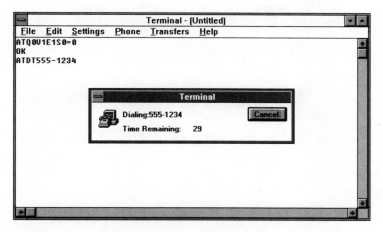

FIGURE 26-8. *The Terminal window while your computer is dialing.*

TRANSFERRING A TEXT FILE

During a communications session with another computer, you might want to transmit or receive text contained in a file. A text file is a file that contains only characters that can be typed using the keyboard. It can't contain any special formatting such as italics, underlining, or double-spacing. The Notepad application creates only text files. The Write application creates formatted files. You can, however, save a document created in Write as a text file. In Write, choose the Save As command from the File menu and select Text Files (∗.TXT) from the Save File as Type drop-down list box.

Receiving a Text File

When you're ready to receive a text file, choose the Receive Text File command from the Transfers menu (Alt,T,R). The Receive Text File dialog box, shown in Figure 26-9, works like a Save As dialog box. Several special features of this dialog box are noted in the figure.

After you finish filling in the dialog box and choose OK, Terminal displays a status bar at the bottom of the window. The status bar, shown in Figure 26-10, gives you information about the file and contains buttons for convenient control of the transfer.

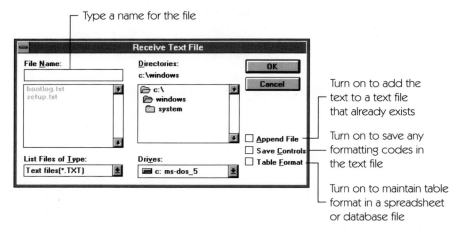

FIGURE 26-9. *The Receive Text File dialog box.*

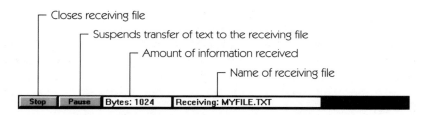

FIGURE 26-10. *The status bar while Terminal is receiving a text file.*

When it is receiving a text file, Terminal stores in the file everything that is displayed in its window (including whatever you type). To transfer text from the other computer to your computer, send the commands that display the text. For example, if you're connected to a UNIX computer, you might type *cat NewStaff* to display the contents of the file NewStaff. Or, for an article from an online service, you would type the command to read the article. To stop receiving, choose the Stop button on the status bar or choose the Stop command from the Transfers menu (Alt,T,O). Figure 26-11 shows a text file being received from the online service CompuServe. After you choose the Receive Text File command, everything that appears on the screen is saved in the text file SMALL.TXT. (SMALL.TXT is the filename you typed in the Receive Text File dialog box.) As you can see, so far 3,072 bytes have been received. When you've finished your communications session, you can view the information again in the receiving text file.

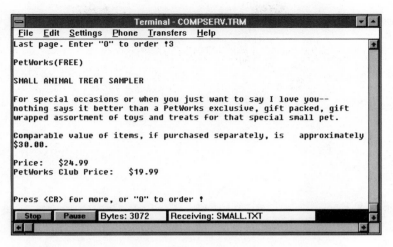

FIGURE 26-11. *Receiving a text file in Terminal.*

Viewing a Text File

To view a text file you have received, choose the View Text File command from the Transfers menu (Alt,T,V). The View Text File dialog box, shown in Figure 26-12, works like an Open dialog box.

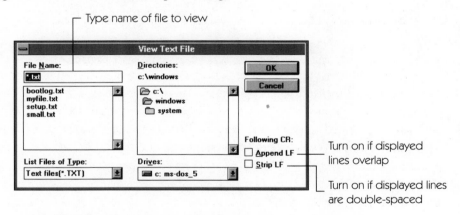

FIGURE 26-12. *The View Text File dialog box.*

After you choose the name of the file you want to see and choose OK, Terminal displays the file along with a status bar. The progress indicator on the status bar lets you see how much of the file has been displayed. If the file is long, Terminal scrolls the window to make room for the new text. To see the text before it scrolls out of view, choose the Pause button on the status bar. Choose the Resume button to display more text.

Sending a Text File

If your computer connection requires a long-distance telephone call (or if the other computer charges a connection fee based on time connected), you'll want to keep your connection time as short as possible. One way to send text as quickly as possible is to compose the text before connecting and then send the text in a file.

To send a text file, choose the Send Text File command from the Transfers menu (Alt,T,S). As you can see in Figure 26-13, the Send Text File dialog box works like an Open dialog box.

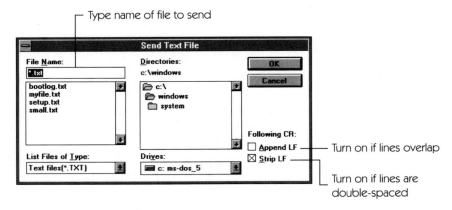

FIGURE 26-13. *The Send Text File dialog box.*

After you specify the name of the file, choose OK to send the text file to the other computer. You'll see a status bar, which lets you track the progress of the transfer.

If There Are Problems

In most cases, you should be able to transfer text files between computers without worry. If your text transfers do not run smoothly, choose the Text Transfers command from the Settings menu (Alt,S,X). If you just need to set the line-break column for text you are sending, stick with the Standard Flow Control setting. With Standard Flow Control selected, turn on the Word Wrap

Outgoing Text at Column check box, and change the column number. You'll need to change this setting for files that were created with a word processor that doesn't put a carriage return at the end of each line. The default value, 79, works well in most cases. If text transfers are botched up in other ways, choose one of the other two Flow Control settings. Notice that the text in the middle of the dialog box changes for each Flow Control setting. Figure 26-14 shows you the three versions of the Text Transfers dialog box.

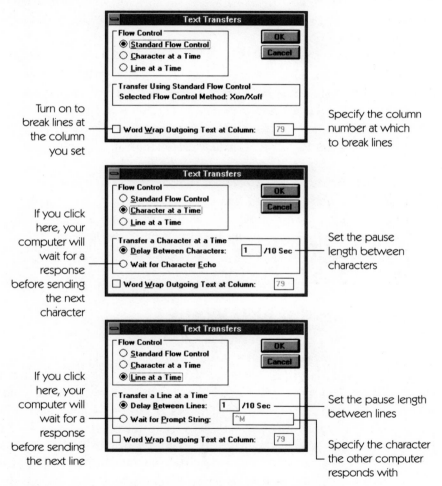

FIGURE 26-14. *The Text Transfers dialog boxes for Standard Flow Control, Character at a Time, and Line at a Time settings.*

Using the Clipboard with Terminal

To speed the process of sending pieces of text (instead of entire files) to another computer, you can copy text to the Clipboard and then have Terminal send the contents of the Clipboard to another computer.

To copy text to the Clipboard, select the text from a file in another application (or in the Terminal window), and choose the Copy command from the Edit menu (Alt,E,C or Ctrl+C). To select all the text available in the Terminal window, choose the Select All command from the Edit menu (Alt,E,A).

After you copy text to the Clipboard, you can "paste" it to the other computer. To send the Clipboard contents to the other computer, choose the Paste command from Terminal's Edit menu (Alt,E,P or Ctrl+V). The pasted text appears in the Terminal window and is sent to the other computer.

Instead of the two-step process of copy and paste, you can use one command to resend selected text in the Terminal window to another computer. Select the text in the Terminal window, and then choose the Send command from the Edit menu (Alt,E,N or Ctrl+Shift+Ins). When you choose the Send command, Terminal copies the text onto the Clipboard and then sends the Clipboard contents to the other computer.

TRANSFERRING A BINARY FILE

If you want to transfer program files or text files that contain formatted text, you must transfer the file as a binary file. Binary files contain only 1s and 0s, and in this form binary files can contain any kind of information. To transfer binary files, you must set up Terminal to match the transfer protocol setup of the other computer. (The protocol specifies the way a computer checks that the information is reaching it correctly.) To set up Terminal to transfer binary files, choose the Binary Transfers command from the Settings menu (Alt,S,B). Terminal offers two protocols: XModem/CRC and Kermit. XModem/CRC is faster than Kermit and so should be used whenever possible. Select the protocol from the Binary Transfers dialog box, and choose OK. The Binary Transfers dialog box is shown in Figure 26-15.

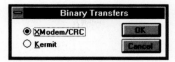

FIGURE 26-15. *The Binary Transfers dialog box.*

Sending a Binary File

Sending and receiving binary files is similar to sending and receiving text files. The most visible difference is that Terminal does not display the binary file during transfer. The status bar does appear, as shown in Figure 26-16.

FIGURE 26-16. *The Terminal window and status bar during a binary file transfer.*

Before another computer can receive a binary file, that computer must be set up for receiving. Sometimes a person must be present to set it up. In other cases, the computer allows you to set it up by typing a special command. Ask the person with whom you're communicating what steps must be taken.

When the other computer is ready, choose the Send Binary File command from the Transfers menu (Alt,T,B). The Send Binary File dialog box works like an Open dialog box. Specify the name of the file, and choose the OK button to start the transfer.

For example, suppose you want to send the binary file RIBBONS.BMP to a XENIX computer. Figure 26-16 shows the window during the transfer. In this case, the other computer allows you to set it up for transfer. You can see at the top of the window that the other computer first asks whether you want to download (receive) a file or upload (send) a file. After you type *2* to signify that you want to send a file, the other computer prompts you to specify the type of file you will be sending and the name of the file. When the other computer prompts you to start the transfer, choose the Send Binary File command from the Transfers menu.

Receiving a Binary File

You can ask a person at the other computer to send you a binary file, or (if possible) you can type a command in Terminal that causes the other computer to send the file. After the other computer begins sending the file, choose the Receive Binary File command from the Transfers menu (Alt,T,F). The Receive Binary File dialog box works like a Save As dialog box. After you specify a name for the file and choose OK, Terminal begins receiving the file. It displays a status bar to show you the progress.

For example, suppose you want to receive a file from the online service CompuServe. Figure 26-17 shows you the portion of the communications session that sets up the other computer (CompuServe) so that it sends the file. First CompuServe asks whether you want to download (receive) the file. Then it asks what protocol you will use. Because the only protocol in the list supported by Terminal is XMODEM, you would type *1* to choose the XMODEM protocol.

Figure 26-18 shows you the Terminal window during the transfer of the file. You can see that CompuServe prompts you to start the transfer. You should respond to that prompt by choosing Receive Binary File from the Transfers menu.

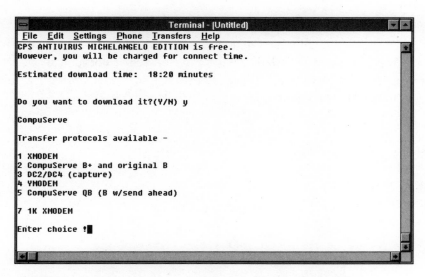

FIGURE 26-17. *Setting up to receive a binary file from CompuServe.*

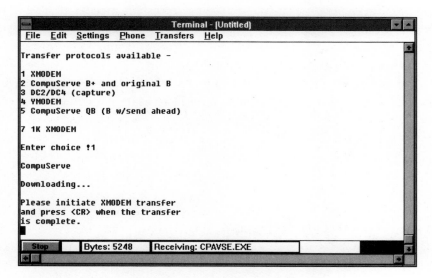

FIGURE 26-18. *Receiving a binary file from CompuServe.*

HANGUP

The Hangup command on the Phone menu closes the telephone connection. Choose this command when you have completed your communications session. The Terminal window will display the hang-up codes you set for your modem in the Modem Commands dialog box.

Chapter 27

Having Fun
with Solitaire

In Chapter 4, "Using the Mouse," you played Minesweeper to help you learn to handle the mouse (and to have fun, too). In this chapter you'll learn to play the other game that comes with the Windows operating system: Solitaire. Solitaire is based on the Klondike version of the solitaire card game. In this version, however, you can choose to draw three cards at a time or one card at a time, and you can choose different scoring methods. Like Minesweeper, Solitaire is a game that helps you learn to use the mouse more skillfully. It helps you master clicking, double-clicking, and dragging. The Solitaire icon appears in the Games group window in Program Manager. The Solitaire window is shown in Figure 27-1.

The object of the game is to place all the cards in order, from ace through king, in their own suits on the suit stacks. Secondarily, the object is to achieve the best score you can. The more skilled you become in the game, the higher your score will be. In the basic scoring setup of this game, you lose points for taking extra time to complete the game. In another scoring setup, you carry over your score (kept in dollars) to subsequent games. With luck and skill, you can build quite a nest egg.

PLAYING THE GAME

When you start Solitaire, the first deal of the cards happens automatically, as shown in Figure 27-1. After the first game, you deal the cards by opening the Game menu and choosing the Deal command (Alt,G,D). You can request a new deal at any time during a game, even at the beginning.

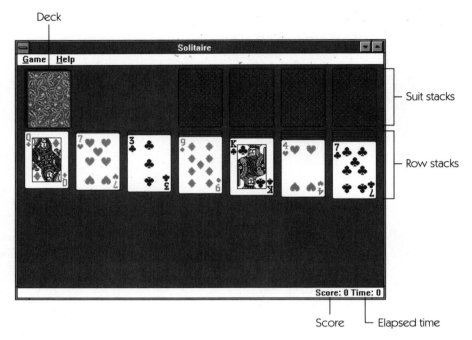

FIGURE 27-1. *The initial Solitaire window.*

After the cards are dealt, you start to play. You move cards in the row stacks by placing a card from one row stack on top of the last card in another row stack. The card you place there has to be less in value by one and of alternate color. For example, if the last card in a row stack is a black 8 (spades or clubs), you can place on top of it a red 7 (hearts or diamonds) from another row stack. If the card you are moving has other cards on top of it in its row stack, those cards are moved over as well, keeping the sequence of cards intact. You can learn by trying it out. Solitaire won't let you place a card incorrectly—or cheat! Here's a hint: Move as many cards in the row stacks as possible before you start playing the cards from the deck. Figure 27-2 shows what the stacks look like after several plays.

To place one card on top of another, drag the card until it covers the destination card. Don't worry about positioning the card exactly. After you release the mouse button, Solitaire will position the card. When you play a card from the top of the row stacks, you uncover the face-down cards underneath. To

274

turn over a card in a row stack, click the back of the card. Eventually you might empty a row stack to reveal the "table top" underneath. When you do, you can move any king into the empty row stack.

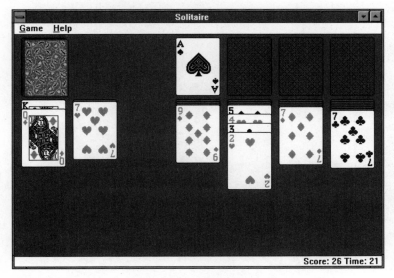

FIGURE 27-2. *The row stacks after several plays.*

When you encounter an ace of any suit, place it in an empty slot above the row stacks. This creates a suit stack. (You can place the ace in any available slot. The slots are not assigned to particular suits.) Then build up the suit stack by moving the next higher card of the same suit from either the row stacks or the deck. For example, if you've created a suit stack with an ace of spades, you can cover it with an exposed 2 of spades. The 3 of spades can be placed next, and so on.

Fast-Building Suit Stacks

Normally, you would drag a card to its suit stack. A faster way to put any card on its suit stack is to double-click the card. Solitaire places it on the proper suit stack.

When you have made all the available plays in the row stacks, you need to turn over cards from the deck. You do this by clicking the top card on the deck, as shown in Figure 27-3. In the initial set up of Solitaire, three cards will turn over.

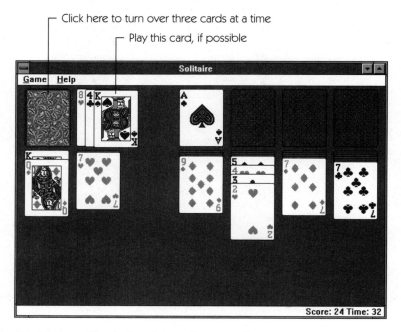

FIGURE 27-3. *The deck and turned-over cards.*

If you can play the top turned-over card, drag it to the appropriate suit stack or row stack. Then try to play the next turned-over card in the pile. If you can't play the top turned-over card, click the deck again to turn over more cards from the deck.

After you've turned over all the cards in the deck, you can return the deck to its ''face down'' position by clicking the area in which the deck was originally placed. See Figure 27-4.

You can turn the deck as many times as you want. Of course, after a while, there are no possible plays left and continuing to run through the deck is fruitless. It's time to deal again to start a new game.

Click here to return deck to "face down" position

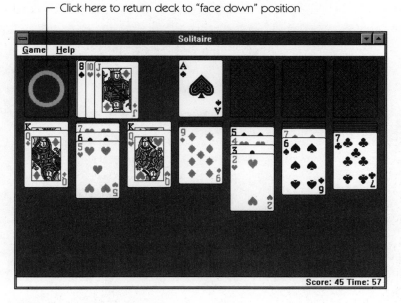

FIGURE 27-4. *The deck all turned over.*

Reversing a Bad Play

Sometimes during play you overlook a good move, only to notice it just as you do something else. Like other applications, Solitaire has an Undo command, which is located on the Game menu (Alt,G,U). The Undo command in Solitaire reverses only your last action. After you undo a play, the Undo command is not available until you make another play.

Outline Dragging

You might notice after playing one or two cards that the cards drag slowly and sometimes jerkily. You can speed up and smooth out dragging by turning on outline dragging. *With outline dragging turned on, you drag only an empty box to the destination; when you release the mouse button, the card appears on the stack.*

To turn on outline dragging, choose the Options command from the Game menu (Alt,G,O). See the Options dialog box in Figure 27-6.

Scoring

When you first start playing Solitaire, the game is set to the Standard scoring option. Figure 27-5 shows you how points are earned and lost during play. If you finish a game by placing all the cards in the suit stacks, you receive bonus points. The faster you finish, the higher the point total.

Points	For
10	Each card you move to the suit stacks
5	Each card you move from the deck to the row stacks
-15	Each card you move from the suit stacks to the playing stacks
-20	For Draw Three option, each pass through the deck after three passes
-100	For Draw One option, each pass through the deck after one pass
-2	For every 10 consecutive seconds of idle time

FIGURE 27-5. *The Standard scoring in Solitaire.*

CHANGING GAMES

The initial setup of Solitaire keeps score with points, one game at a time. When you turn over the deck, you turn over three cards at a time. Also, the game is timed and uses Standard scoring (including points deducted for slow play). You can change these settings by choosing the Options command from the Game menu (Alt,G,O). See Figure 27-6.

FIGURE 27-6. *The Options dialog box.*

The Options dialog box gives you the option to turn one card at a time when you click the deck. It also gives you the option of Vegas scoring or no scoring at all. In Vegas scoring you play for dollars: $52 is deducted from your score when you begin playing the game, and $5 is awarded for each card you move to the suit stacks. In Vegas scoring you get three passes through the deck when you choose the Draw Three option, and you get only one pass through the deck when you choose the Draw One option.

The Options dialog box also contains check boxes that allow you to turn scoring and timing on and off. You can even turn off the status bar that shows score and time at the bottom of the Solitaire window.

By the way, if you change the number of cards to turn over, the type of scoring, or the timing in the Options dialog box, Solitaire deals a new game. It's best not to change those settings in the middle of a game.

GIVING YOUR DECK A DIFFERENT LOOK

Solitaire offers a selection of 12 deck designs when you choose the Deck command from the Game menu (Alt,G,C). You'll see your choices displayed in the Select Card Back dialog box, shown in Figure 27-7. Choose a card design with the mouse or arrow keys.

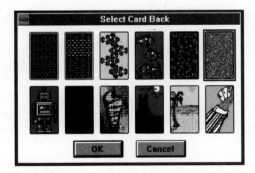

FIGURE 27-7. *The Select Card Back dialog box.*

You can switch card designs in the middle of a game without affecting the game at all. Some of the designs have small motions built into them. Some of these motions are continuous, some are intermittent. Keep your eyes peeled!

Chapter 28

Changing Windows with the Windows Setup Application

Your first exposure to setting up Windows was probably when you installed the Windows operating system on your computer with the Windows Setup program. If someone else set up Windows for you, then you haven't yet had to set up anything. In either case, you'll be glad to know that you don't have to start all over with the Windows Setup program when you want to change Windows. You can use the Windows Setup application, whose icon is located in the Main group window of Program Manager.

After you install Windows, the Windows Setup application helps you change system settings (display, keyboard, mouse, network), set up applications already on your hard disk, and add or remove Windows components. If an additional file has to be copied to your computer in this process, the Windows Setup application will prompt you to insert the relevant disk from the Windows package into your floppy-disk drive. Then Windows Setup copies the file for you. The Windows Setup window is shown in Figure 28-1.

Windows Setup	
Options　**Help**	
Display:	VGA
Keyboard:	Enhanced 101 or 102 key US and Non US
Mouse:	Microsoft, or IBM PS/2
Network:	Microsoft LAN Manager (version 2.0 Basic)

The computer's current system settings

FIGURE 28-1. *The Windows Setup window.*

CHANGING SYSTEM SETTINGS

Windows system settings apply to the display, keyboard, mouse, and network you have installed. As a rule, you won't need to change these settings. However, if you get a new, higher-resolution display, a new keyboard, or a new mouse, or if you change networks, you will need to also change Windows' system settings.

Windows Setup displays your current system settings in its window. (See Figure 28-1.) To change settings, open the Options menu and choose the Change System Settings command (Alt,O,C). The dialog box is shown in Figure 28-2. It has a drop-down list box for each setting.

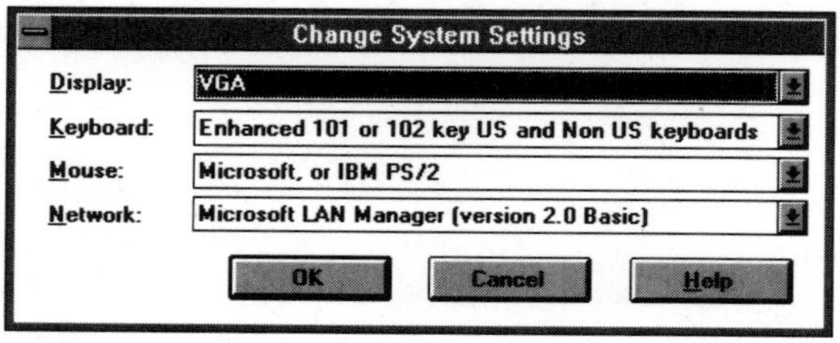

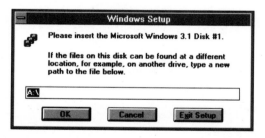

FIGURE 28-2. *The Change System Settings dialog box.*

Select the new settings, and choose OK. Windows Setup displays a message box if it needs to copy a particular file. Figure 28-3 shows an example of one such message box.

FIGURE 28-3. *A message box that asks for a disk or for a file's location.*

After you choose OK and the new file is copied, the new setting appears in the Windows Setup window.

SETTING UP APPLICATIONS

Windows Setup makes it easy for you to add applications to Program Manager. Choose the Set Up Applications command from the Options menu (Alt,O,S). You will see the dialog box shown in Figure 28-4.

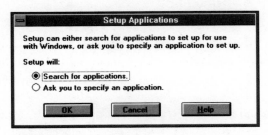

FIGURE 28-4. *The first Setup Applications dialog box.*

You can go ahead and leave the "Search for applications" option selected. Windows Setup won't make any changes to Windows without your approval. After you choose OK, Windows Setup brings up a dialog box that asks where you would like it to search for applications. See Figure 28-5.

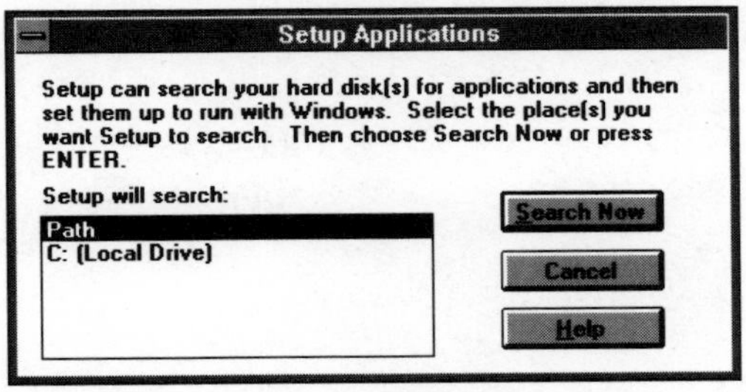

FIGURE 28-5. *The second Setup Applications dialog box.*

One option in Figure 28-5 tells Windows Setup to look for applications in the *path*. The path refers to a group of directories in which your computer customarily searches for files. This group is determined by a setting called *PATH* in a file called *AUTOEXEC.BAT*. The second option tells Windows Setup to search all the directories on your hard disk. After you select an option and choose Search Now, Windows Setup looks for applications and eventually displays the third Setup Applications dialog box, shown in Figure 28-6.

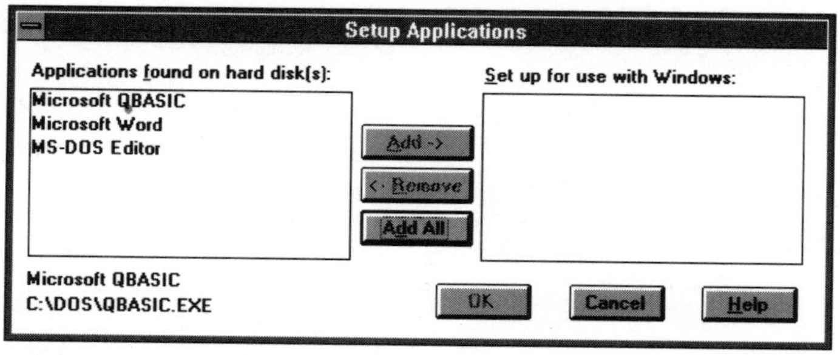

FIGURE 28-6. *The third Setup Applications dialog box.*

You can select as many applications as you want from the list on the left side of the dialog box by clicking each one. (To select or deselect an application with the keyboard, press the Tab key to move to the list box. A dotted box appears. Press the up or down arrow key to move the dotted box to the application you want to select, and then press the spacebar to highlight it.) As you select or move the dotted box to each application, Setup displays the application's name and directory in the lower left corner of the dialog box. If you accidentally select an application you don't want to add, click it again to deselect it. When you select the first of the applications you want to add to Program Manager, the Add button will no longer be grayed. Choose the Add button after you've selected all the applications you want. The applications will then be listed on the right side of the dialog box, as shown in Figure 28-7.

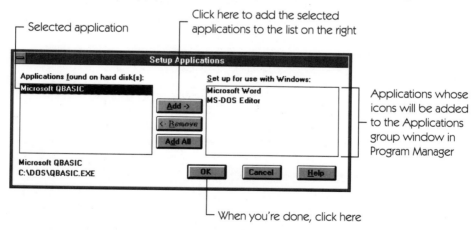

FIGURE 28-7. *The third Setup Applications dialog box with some applications added to the list on the right.*

Choose OK. Setup adds the applications' icons to the Applications group window in Program Manager.

You can also remove applications from the list on the right side of the dialog box in Figure 28-7. Select the applications first. The Remove button will no longer be grayed. Choose the Remove button.

ADDING OR REMOVING WINDOWS COMPONENTS

When you installed Windows, you had a choice between Express Setup and Custom Setup. Chapter 2, "Installing Windows," recommended that you choose Express Setup. If you did, you most likely have a number of Windows files on your hard disk that you never use. You can safely remove some of these files to recover disk space for your work files. On the other hand, if you chose Custom Setup, you might find that you now need to add some files that you excluded during installation. Windows Setup gives you a handy command for adding and removing Windows files. Choose the Add/Remove Windows Components command from the Options menu (Alt,O,A). You'll see the Windows Setup dialog box shown in Figure 28-8.

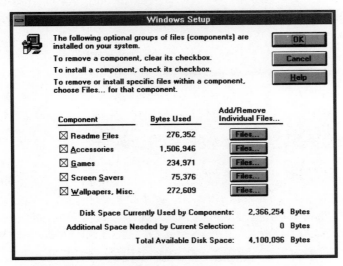

FIGURE 28-8. *The Windows Setup dialog box.*

Windows Setup groups the Windows files into five categories called *components*. To add all the files in a component, turn on its check box. To remove all of a component's files, turn off the check box.

The check boxes are all-or-nothing controls. If you want to decide which individual files to remove or add, choose the Files button for the appropriate component. For example, suppose you plan to use only one screen saver. If you are unlikely to change the screen saver, you can safely remove any screen saver files you won't use. To remove some screen saver files (not wanting to remove them all in this case), choose the Files button beside the Screen Savers component. You will then see the Screen Savers dialog box shown in Figure 28-9.

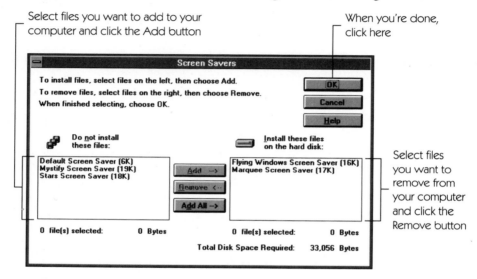

FIGURE 28-9. *The Screen Savers dialog box.*

After you choose OK in the dialog box, you return to the Windows Setup dialog box (Figure 28-8). If you have added or removed some (but not all) files for a component, you'll find that the check box for the component is now gray. You can turn on or off check boxes or choose the Files button for other components you want to change. When you've made all your adjustments, choose OK. For files you want to remove, Setup asks whether you want to remove each file. When you see the first message box, you can choose the Yes to All button to confirm that you want to remove all the files you selected. For files you want to add, Setup asks for the disk that contains the files. (See Figure 28-3 for an example.)

Index

Special Characters

Russell E. Borland earned a bachelor of arts degree from Whitworth College, a master of arts degree from Portland State University, and a Ph.D. degree from the University of Washington. He has been a technical writer for Microsoft Corporation for 12 years and currently resides near Sauk, Washington. Borland is the author of *Working with Word for Windows, Running Word for Windows, Microsoft WordBasic Primer, Microsoft WordBasic Handbook,* and is a coauthor of *Windows 3.1 Companion,* all published by Microsoft Press.

The manuscript for this book was prepared and submitted to Microsoft Press in electronic form. Text files were processed and formatted using Microsoft Word.

Principal editorial compositor: Debbie Kem
Principal proofreader: Deborah Long
Principal typographer: Carolyn Magruder
Interior text designer: Kim Eggleston
Principal illustrator: Lisa Sandburg
Cover designer: Lani Lindell
Cover color separator: Color Control

Text composition by Microsoft Press in Times Roman with display type in Kabel Bold, using the Magna composition system and the Linotronic 300 laser imagesetter.

Printed on recycled paper stock.

More Books from Microsoft Press

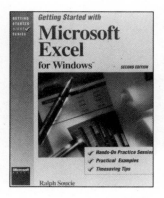

GETTING STARTED WITH MICROSOFT® EXCEL 4 FOR WINDOWS,™ 2nd ed.

Ralph Soucie

If you've never used Microsoft Excel or any other spreadsheet before, GETTING STARTED WITH MICROSOFT EXCEL 4 FOR WINDOWS is the fastest and easiest way to master this popular program. This book is a straightforward, step-by-step guide and example-packed tutorial that is ideal for novice users. You'll quickly pick up the fundamentals of Microsoft Excel's worksheet, charting, database, and macro capabilities with this clear, concise guide. Includes dozens of timesaving tips, practical examples, and screen illustrations.

320 pages, softcover $19.95 ($26.95 Canada)   Available June 1992

RUNNING MICROSOFT EXCEL 4, 3rd ed.

The Cobb Group

The complete reference to Microsoft Excel for Windows—for beginning to advanced users—now updated for version 4.0. Features clear, step-by-step instruction, scores of examples, and detailed reference information. Covers the basics to the finer points of Microsoft Excel's most advanced features.

912 pages, softcover $29.95 ($39.95 Canada)   Available June 1992

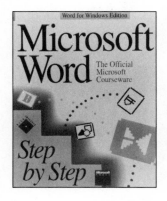

MICROSOFT® WORD FOR WINDOWS™ STEP BY STEP
Version 2

Microsoft Corporation

MICROSOFT WORD FOR WINDOWS STEP BY STEP shows you how Word can make your everyday work easy. Whether you're new to word processing or new to Microsoft Word for Windows, you'll learn to produce professional-quality documents with ease. This timesaving package includes disk-basked tutorials with follow-along lessons and practice exercises. Each lesson includes clear objectives, step-by-step instructions, useful tips, disk-based practice files, plus handy tips, and advice. And the lessons are progressive yet modular, so the novice user can advance from one lesson to the next, and the intermediate user can jump in at any point. This is the perfect training guide for business, classroom, or home use.

292 pages, softcover with one 5¼-inch disk $29.95 ($39.95 Canada)

WORD FOR WINDOWS™ COMPANION, 2nd ed.

The Cobb Group: Mark W. Crane with M. David Stone & Alfred Poor

WORD FOR WINDOWS COMPANION makes Word for Windows easy to learn and use. Regardless of your level of expertise, you'll find a wealth of useful information in this comprehensive resource. It's both an exceptional tutorial for new Word for Windows users and a master reference guide for experienced users. You'll learn basic concepts of word processing, typography, and design to create professional-looking documents with confidence and ease. In addition to detailed explanations, the book offers scores of illustrations, examples, and tips to enhance your productivity. Now updated for version 2.

896 pages, softcover $29.95 ($39.95 Canada)

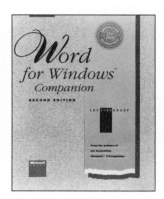

Great Resources for Windows™ 3.1 Users

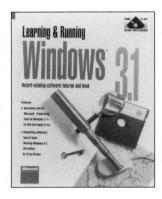

LEARNING & RUNNING WINDOWS™ 3.1
Includes *Microsoft® Productivity Pack for Windows* and *Running Windows 3.1, 3rd ed.*

Microsoft Corporation, Craig Stinson

This is the ideal blending of software and book instruction for users of all levels of experience. If you want to be up and running with Windows 3.1 quickly and easily, this is the place to start. *The Microsoft Productivity Pack for Windows 3.1* (regularly $59.95) combines disk-based lessons with hands-on exercises. RUNNING WINDOWS 3.1 (regularly $27.95) will continue to answer day-to-day questions about Windows long after you've learned the basics from the software tutorial. An unbeatable package at an unbeatable price. Sold separately for $87.90.
560 pages, softcover with one 5 ¹/₂-inch (HD) disk $39.95 ($54.95 Canada)

RUNNING WINDOWS™ 3.1, 3rd ed.
Craig Stinson

Build your confidence and enhance your productivity with Microsoft Windows, quickly and easily, using this hands-on introduction. This Microsoft-authorized edition—for new as well as experienced Windows users—is completely updated and expanded to cover all the new exciting features of version 3.1. You'll find a successful combination of step-by-step tutorials, helpful screen illustrations, expert tips, and real-world examples. Learn how to install and start using Windows 3.1, use applications with Windows, and maximize Windows performance.
560 pages, softcover $27.95 ($37.95 Canada)

WINDOWS™ 3.1 COMPANION
The Cobb Group: Lori L. Lorenz and R. Michael O'Mara with Russell Borland

This bestseller is now completely updated to cover the important new features of version 3.1. Both a step-by-step tutorial and a comprehensive reference, this book is specifically designed to help you quickly find the information you need—moving from the basics to more advanced information. Learn to take advantage of all the extraordinary improvements and added features of version 3.1, including the new, *faster* File Manager; TrueType font; support for multimedia; the improved Program Manager; the faster Printer Manager; automatic network reconnections; the new "drag and drop" feature. The authors include a wealth of expert tips and tricks and great examples to show you how to use Windows more efficiently.
550 pages, softcover $27.95 ($37.95 Canada)

CONCISE GUIDE TO MICROSOFT® WINDOWS™ 3.1
Kris Jamsa

Instant answers to your Windows 3.1 questions! Clear, concise information on all the key Microsoft Windows 3.1 features. For beginning to intermediate users. A great complement to *Windows 3.1 Companion*.
192 pages, softcover $12.95 ($17.95 Canada)